PUFFIN BOOKS

The Fantora Family Photographs

Adèle Geras was born in Jerusalem. Her early childhood was spent in many countries, including North Borneo and the Gambia. She studied French and Spanish at St. Hilda's College, Oxford, and has been a singer, an actress and a teacher of French at a girls' school. She now lives in Manchester with her husband and two daughters.

Another book by Adèle Geras

THE FANTORA FAMILY FILES

The Fantora Family
Photographs

Adèle Geras

Illustrated by Tony Ross

PUFFIN BOOKS

PUFFIN BOOKS

Published by the Penguin Group
Penguin Books Ltd, 27 Wrights Lane, London W8 5TZ, England
Penguin Books USA Inc., 375 Hudson Street, New York, New York 10014, USA
Penguin Books Australia Ltd, Ringwood, Victoria, Australia
Penguin Books Canada Ltd, 10 Alcorn Avenue, Toronto, Ontario, Canada M4V 3B2
Penguin Books (NZ) Ltd, 182–190 Wairau Road, Auckland 10, New Zealand

Penguin Books Ltd, Registered Offices: Harmondsworth, Middlesex, England

First published by Hamish Hamilton Ltd 1993
Published in Puffin Books 1995
1 3 5 7 9 10 8 6 4 2

This book is dedicated to John C, Dennis, Bob, Jan, John M, Jack and Chris: The Offley Gang.

I would also like to thank Marianne Adey, in whose home I first saw the wall of photographs which served as a model for the one at 58, Azalea Avenue.

Contents

I am, at the moment, alone in 58, Azalea Avenue. The other members of the Fantora Family have left for their summer holiday. This year they are spending ten days on the Italian Riviera with our new relations-by-marriage, the Lupinos, and I am not a cat much given to travel. Even a short ride in a car is a disturbance to my routine, and hurtling through the sky in what is, when all is said and done, an enormous metal tube, is my idea of torment.

Although I am alone, I am not lonely. A Narrator is never lonely. As a writer, I have enough tales filling my head to keep me amused forever, and as a cat, I have the capacity for almost infinite dream-filled sleep. I am Ozymandias, the teller of stories, the recounter of the Family History, the Keeper of the Files. The Family call me Ozzy and I allow this, because I am fond of them all. I count it a privilege to be able to tell the world all about them.

I shall begin with an Introduction, so called because I shall be introducing the Family to those people who have not read my previous volume, *The Fantora Family Files*.

1

Introduction

All the Fantoras are unusual in some way. Filomena, the grandmother, can tell the future simply by looking at her knitting. The combinations of colours and stitches give her a good idea of what will be happening in all our lives. (New readers will find Filomena's Colour Chart printed at the end of this book. This will help them in keeping abreast of the narrative, and will save me having to repeat myself.) She will not be called Granny. She lives at the top of the house in a room with sloping ceilings and every day at four o'clock she puts on a purple tracksuit and bounces about on her trampoline, which is kept in the dining room.

Her son, Eddie, who has the greenest fingers in the world, can grow anything anywhere. His shop (The Fantora Greengrocery and Florist's Shop on Buckley Parade) is most successful, because his motto, 'I can get it for you' is nothing less than the truth.

He is married to Rosie, who knows how to fly and how to cook. She has a Magic Potion for every occasion, which is reassuring for us all.

Eddie and Rosie have three children: Bianca, Marco and Francesca. Bianca is ten years old, and can bring anything to life. Her dolls can speak, her ornaments can move and she has even animated illustrations from her books. While she was reading *The Wind in the Willows*, I remember, we had more than a little splashing from the river. The bedroom carpet had to be replaced and Rosie was extremely vexed.

I should perhaps mention at this point that Bianca has brought to life two creatures who used to be ornaments on Francesca's chest-of-drawers. They are called Monkey and Leopard and they follow Francesca all over the house. She is fond of them, and makes a fuss of them and the rest of us quite like them, but find occasionally that they are getting under our feet or being irritating in a mild sort of way. I suppose you could think of them as pets. I, of course, am *not* a pet, but a proper Family member. Most of the time I am relieved that Monkey and Leopard have accompanied Francesca to Italy, but sometimes I feel that even their scuttling and faint squeaking would be welcome.

Marco is nine. He is a quiet child whose gift is invisibility. He enjoys writing poetry, and it is fortunate for him that both his sisters are so fearless, because he is sometimes picked on by larger, noisier boys, who judge a person's worth by how hard they are able to kick a round leather ball.

Francesca, whose name is never shortened, is six, and can change the weather whenever she feels like it. She is stubborn, bossy and more than a little spoilt, but I cannot help loving her. She gets her way rather more often than she should, and this is both because she is extremely charming and also because she can set things on fire with a mere glance if she is angry enough, and fire is to be avoided at all costs.

The Fantoras know all about fire. Auntie Varvara, Eddie's sister, once set her vegeburgers alight, and our precious home, Turrets, was burned to the ground. Auntie Varvara is a vampire and a vegetarian: not an easy combination. She also has the power to move things from place to place simply by thinking about it. She went on holiday to Dracula Country last year and met Remo Lupino, the man who is now her husband and who comes from an illustrious line of Italian werewolves.

This, then, is the Fantora Family and my Introduction is over. The house is empty now: no pinging and twanging of the trampoline, no love songs being warbled by Auntie Varvara in the attic, no delicious smells from Rosie's kitchen, and no children to run up and down stairs and slam doors and quarrel loudly. Above all, no Francesca to hug and stroke me and carry me round in her arms as though I were a young kitten. Still, it is not in my nature to complain.

4

My little luxuries have not been overlooked. Dora Collins from next door puts out my specially prepared chicken twice a day, and cuddles me when I allow it. It was Francesca herself who insisted that I should be regularly cuddled, and Dora tries her best, although she always looks a little embarrassed. I am sometimes rather naughty and ungrateful and try to avoid her strokings and cluckings by pretending to be fast asleep.

'You must talk to Ozzy as well,' Francesca had told Dora more than once before leaving, and Dora does her best.

'How are you, Ozzy?' 'You keeping well, Ozzy?' 'How's life treating you, Ozzy?' is about the limit of her chat. Anyone would agree that it is somewhat less than sparkling, but she does mean well. Once in a rare moment of confession she admitted, 'I *do* feel silly, talking to a cat, Ozzy. No offence of course. Still, I promised Francesca.'

There is nothing more to be said. There are those who feel silly talking to cats, and those who understand that talking to cats is the very acme and pinnacle of conversational achievement. Dora Collins has many sterling qualities, and I am tolerant by nature, and forgive her. However, I am often to be found curled up with my eyes firmly closed when she appears.

I go in and out of the house through the catflap, although of course I prefer doors to be opened for me. The catflap is an excellent device, but a little racy and youthful for my tastes. Filomena has spread a woollen shawl on Francesca's bed. This shawl has been specially knitted to bring on sweet dreams. I have everything I could possibly want. It is simply that the silence in every room is so loud.

As a cat who has lived through many summers, I comfort myself that this one also will turn into autumn, and that these next few days will go by very quickly. As a writer, I have an even greater source of comfort: my stories of the Family. The last few months have been eventful for all of us. One glance at the Family Wall proves it beyond doubt.

The Family Wall was Rosie's idea. She had seen such a wall at the house of a friend, and had decided at once to copy it.

'It's just the thing,' she said, 'for a space where no one ever puts anything interesting.'

'What is?' said Filomena, who had been listening less than attentively.

'Lots and lots of framed photographs,' said Rosie, 'all up the wall beside the stairs. Then every time anyone goes up or down, they can look at fascinating snapshots. Why, you could have our whole history up on one wall.'

'Won't it look, well, crowded?' Bianca asked.

'Yes, of course it will,' said Rosie. 'That's just the point. Because it's so crowded, your eye picks out something different to look at every time. If there were only one photograph there, in the middle of a wide, white wall, you'd be forced to look at that, don't you see?'

'I suppose so,' said Eddie. He did not sound convinced.

'I think it's a wonderful idea,' said Auntie Varvara. 'Amazingly artistic. I shall even let you have the one of me being bathed as a baby.'

And so the photographs were chosen for the Wall, frames were ordered, everything was hung, and now, as you walk up the stairs to the landing, on your left is what Auntie Varvara assures us is called 'a montage'.

'I know about such things,' she said. 'Don't forget I did an Introduction to Modern Art course five years ago, and I'm not frightened to use a French word when I have to.'

To me, the Wall is a patchwork, made up of pictures both in black and white and in colour. I myself am in many of the photographs. You can admire me on Francesca's lap, on the balcony at Turrets as a young kitten, and in Family groups of one kind and another. I can be seen looking frisky, cuddlesome, sinister, dashing, witty. I am there in all my infinite variety. My favourite photograph, however, is one of the most recent additions to the Wall. I am posed on a purple velvet cushion, and the colour contrasts pleasingly with my black fur. I am in what I call my Sphinx position, gazing straight at the camera. I look

7

regal. No, I look (and a Narrator should never indulge in false modesty) positively imperial. This photograph, like all photographs, has an interesting story behind it, a story about me, and I shall reveal it in the fullness of time. At the moment, the only clue I am prepared to drop is this: one day at breakfast, a few months ago, I noticed Bianca and Marco looking very carefully at a particular page in the newspaper, and then peering equally carefully at me. Then, later in the day, I caught Bianca cutting something out of the newspaper. Later still, I overheard her and Marco giggling and whispering in a corner. They kept eyeing me, as though they were seeing me for the very first time. Are you curious to know what was happening? You will have to wait patiently until I choose to reveal more.

This was a short digression, and I shall now return to my account of the Family Wall. The photographs go back as far as Filomena's own grandmother, and the most recent ones show us all at Auntie Varvara's wedding, from which, I may say, I am only just beginning to recover. I will save recounting the events of that momentous occasion to a time when I feel stronger. At the moment, from where I am sitting in a small patch of sunlight on the third step up, my eye is caught by a misty photograph of Auntie Varvara dressed in a floating arrangement of bits of material, with some kind of garland low over her brow, and bunches of flowers pinned to lengths of ribbon and tied round her wrists and ankles. From the way she is holding her arms above her head and looking sideways soulfully, you can tell she is supposed to be dancing. I recall Auntie Varvara's Modern Dance period very well. It was only a few years ago. She used to do what she called 'barre exercises' in the bathroom. The heated towel rail was exactly the right height, and as long as Auntie Varvara remembered to cover it with a towel before touching it, her fingers were safe. There was, however, the odd howl of pain from time to time, and Eddie complained he could never get into the bathroom to shave. Luckily, the Modern Dance period lasted no longer than a few months.

'I'm too tall,' said Auntie Varvara, 'and besides, I feel I need something a little more stimulating. Perhaps I should try Disco Dancing.'

She did not try Disco Dancing. She did not mention it again, and it is only this photograph of her as (I think) a wood nymph to testify to poor Auntie Varvara's short-lived devotion to Terpsichore, the Muse of the Dance.

Francesca's ballet photograph is quite different. There is a story to be told about her Dancing Display, and I, Ozzy Fantora, am going to tell it now.

I can hear your objections even as I write. How, you are saying to yourself, can a cat who

9

rarely leaves his own territory bring to life dancing classes, rehearsals, and performances of which he has no personal experience? How does he know what the places look like? I will not deny that it is a kind of magic. The main ingredient of the magic is imagination. I have to think myself into the situation of the characters in my story. I am helped by many things: other people's accounts of events, and their descriptions, what I have seen on television or read of similar situations, and so forth. In other words, I put a story together in just the same way that Rosie arranged the Family Wall: a picture here and a picture there (I can hear Auntie Varvara murmur 'montage'!) which add up in the end to what I hope is an elegant and harmonious whole. This is a long story, so I shall tell it in two parts. Part One is called 'The Dancing Class'.

The Dancing Class

Francesca started attending the Otter Street Primary School in January. I can recall her first morning as though it were yesterday. Bianca and Marco normally slurped through their cornflakes in a state that in many ways resembled sleep, but on Francesca's first day, they were unusually talkative. They showered their poor little sister with advice.

'Don't draw attention to yourself. No snowstorms at playtime.'

11

'Don't remind people that you've got a brother and sister further up the school. They'll think you're showing off.'

'Don't show off.'

'Don't tell anyone you're Filomena's grandchild.'

'Don't dress too warmly. The heating's always on too high.'

Francesca listened calmly to everything they said, and smiled sweetly.

'Everyone knows I'm related to you and Filomena. There can't be two families called Fantora. But I'll try not to fiddle with the weather at first.' She bit into her toast. 'Anyway,' she went on, 'I'll be fine, because the knitting says so, doesn't it, Filomena?'

'It does,' said Filomena. 'Nothing but rows and rows of evenly-spaced stocking stitch in a delightfully happy shade of apple green for new beginnings.'

'So there's nothing to be nervous about,' Francesca said, and went off to school with Bianca and Marco. There was a poignant moment, just before she left the house, when she buried her nose in my fur and said, 'Oh, Ozzy, I shan't see you till four o'clock. I'll miss you so much. Will you think of me?'

I promised to think of her, and I did. I thought of her constantly. At her old school, the day finished at twelve o'clock for the infant classes, and I'd become used to having her at home by lunchtime. When the clock ticked round to noon and there was no Francesca to feed, a sort of restlessness ran through the whole house. Monkey and Leopard were nibbling listlessly at one of the succulents growing in pots on the windowsill, and Rosie didn't even notice. She was rustling through the newspaper at the kitchen table.

'There's a job advertised here,' she announced to Auntie Varvara and Filomena, who were drifting more or less aimlessly around the kitchen, drinking unwanted cups of coffee. 'I shall apply for it. It will be better than rattling round an empty house, waiting for the children to come home.'

'Yes, a job would be lovely,' Auntie Varvara murmured. She had taken to murmuring rather a lot since falling in love last September. 'I would look for one myself, only I simply haven't the time. There's so much to do before the wedding.'

It seemed to me that Auntie Varvara's main occupation at this time was the leafing through of magazines. 'Leafing through' is perhaps not the best way to describe it. No, as a Narrator it is my duty to be accurate, and Auntie Varvara was studying these publications, poring over every page with the devotion of a medieval monk at his prayer book. From the glossy pictures in *Bridal Bounty* and *Wedding Wonderland* she gleaned priceless information on such subjects as what were the most fashionable fabrics for the modern wedding dress, how to run up tasteful table decorations, and where to seat such awkward members of the family as the groom's second cousin four times removed.

To return to Francesca's first day at school ... even Filomena, who was never at a loose end (you will forgive the pun, I'm sure!) began to find bumpy little patches of discontented moss-stitch showing up in her work. But, 'We'll all get used to the house being empty,' she said. 'In a couple of weeks. It was just the same when Bianca and Marco first went to school full-time. Still, I do think a job for you, Rosie, is a splendid idea. I feel like a new woman since starting mine.'

Filomena goes into Otter Street School every Wednesday morning, that is all, but as she confessed to me once, 'It gives a shape to the week.'

As for me, I couldn't settle to my after-lunch snooze. I found myself wondering and wondering how Francesca's first day had been.

She told me all about it after tea, when Bianca and Marco were too busy to listen, Filomena was trampolining and Rosie was cooking the evening meal.

'I've got a friend, Ozzy. A really proper lovely friend with brown curly hair and blue eyes. She's called Polly. Polly Roberts, and guess what? She lives in the big white house on the corner of Sparrow Lane and Gale Street.'

I purred my delight at Francesca's happiness, but wondered whether she might not become a little dissatisfied with 58, Azalea Avenue when she was invited to look at life in the big white house.

The children had been making up stories about the inhabitants of this house for many years, and now here was Francesca on her first day at school, bosom friends with the little girl who lived there. I was very curious to learn all I could about the denizens of such a magnificent residence. According to Francesca, appearances were deceptive. The big white house turned out to be in need of a dusting ('I wrote my name on the mirror in the downstairs loo,' Francesca giggled). Mrs Roberts was one of those vague mothers whose thoughts are fixed on more important things than food, and Mr Roberts was permanently hidden behind something, usually a newspaper or a pile of books. Polly, however, was exactly what Francesca required of a friend. That is to say, she was very pretty and she generally agreed with Francesca. Filomena's knitting was showing thin stripes in two colours.

'That's very good,' she told us. 'That shows a nice friendship. Only two colours and pleasantly close together.'

A few days after the beginning of term, Francesca told us at supper, 'Polly goes to ballet lessons. It's ace, she says. They all meet in St

Christopher's Church Hall on Tuesday afternoons at five o'clock, and they have lovely satin shoes and the big girls stand on their toes and they're having a Dancing Display in April. Could I go? To the class? I'm sure they'd have me. The teacher's name is Madame Vera. She's Russian.'

An interesting discussion then began about why ballet teachers were so often Russian.

'I expect,' said Bianca, 'it's because the Russians are famous for ballet dancing. And besides, it's dead glamorous, having a foreign name.'

'We've got a foreign name,' said Marco. 'Are we glamorous?'

'I'm going to be,' said Francesca. 'When I grow up. Definitely.'

Auntie Varvara was looking around expectantly, waiting for someone to remark upon her glamour. No one did, though, so she went back to dissecting the split-pea cutlet that lay on the plate in front of her. Francesca brought the conversation back to ballet classes.

'May I go?' she asked again. 'I could go with Polly, the Tuesday after next. Please?'

Rosie sighed. 'Eddie, what do you think?'

Eddie frowned. 'If it'll make Francesca happy, it's fine with me,' he said in the end.

He had long ago learned the wisdom of being on Francesca's side in any battle of wills. Being on the other side sometimes meant one of your more precious possessions being slightly scorched.

Francesca rewarded her father with a dazzling smile.

'I shall telephone Madame Vera tomorrow then,' said Rosie, 'and arrange it all.'

She was as good as her word. She also decided that Auntie Varvara, (who, after all had had what she called 'Dancing Experience') should be in charge of decking Francesca out in all the required outfits.

I am not a Narrator much given to exaggeration, so I ask you to believe me when I tell you that equipping an army for combat overseas would have been an easy task by comparison with Getting Francesca Ready.

The special leotards which Madame Vera insisted on could only be obtained in a shop that happened to be two bus-rides away.

'Let's go in the car,' Francesca said, 'after school tomorrow.'

'I'm taking the car to the Hypermarket tomorrow,' said Rosie. 'I could take you on Saturday.'

Francesca said, 'Oh, I can't wait till Saturday. I want to go tomorrow. What about Dad's van?'

I could detect the tiniest wobble in her lower lip.

'Delivering,' Eddie said.

'Never mind, dear,' said Auntie Varvara brightly. 'We'll go by bus. We'll be fine.'

Auntie Varvara has never learned to drive and feels a little guilty about it.

When they reached the shop, the leotards in Francesca's size were the wrong colour, and the correctly-coloured ones were too big or too small, and so the garments had to be ordered from another branch. Then the tension mounted daily as we waited to see: would the leotards be delivered in time for the first class? Most readers enjoy a little suspense, but too much is a strain, so I shall tell you at once: they arrived in good time.

Next, Francesca had to have a small pink suitcase. It had to be round, like a little hatbox, and it had to have a picture of a ballerina on the lid.

'Six shops!' sighed Auntie Varvara, sinking into a chair after a Saturday spent suitcase-hunting. 'My feet! I feel I shall hobble until my dying day.'

The shoes, the ribbons, the hairnet (to cover the bun that had to be worn by all girls with long hair), even the correct brush and comb: we fought through them all and we lived to tell the tale.

On the Monday evening before Francesca's first class, Auntie Varvara said, 'Well, I never thought we'd do it in time, but we have.'

At that point, the telephone rang. It was Polly. When Francesca came back into the lounge after speaking to her friend, she had the grace to look ashamed.

'I'm sorry,' she said. 'I forgot. Polly's just reminded me. I have to have a cardigan that crosses over at the front. In black or white.'

Auntie Varvara let out an involuntary wail.

'You're not having time off school,' said Rosie, 'to go traipsing round the shops searching for crossover cardigans, and that's that.'

Filomena coughed gently. 'Aren't you all overlooking something?'

No one answered, so Filomena continued, 'You are. You're overlooking me. A cardigan in Francesca's size will take me no time at all. Would you like black or white, Francesca?'

'You are the best and cleverest granny in the world!' cried Francesca. 'Thank you!'

She flung her arms around Filomena and hugged her.

'I accept the compliment,' Filomena said. 'But a little less emphasis on the 'Granny' please! Now, would you like black or white?'

'Black,' said Francesca.

'A very sensible choice,' said Filomena. 'Practical and smart.'

'Better than smart,' said Francesca. 'Glamorous!'

I kept Filomena company as she knitted through the dark hours. I cannot truthfully say I followed every stitch, but I did take up my position that night in one of her wool baskets. My eyes insisted on closing, my head *would* tuck itself under my front paws without my really intending it to, but I looked up every now and again, and each time I did, I saw Filomena's fingers whirring through the air, and the ball of black wool on her lap becoming smaller and smaller.

'How fortunate that I need so little sleep,' she said to me at dawn, as she showed me the finished pieces of Francesca's cardigan. 'I shall sew these together today.' She was whispering, because everyone else in the house was still in bed. 'I think,' she continued, 'that I might close my eyes for a few moments now, Ozzy, if you don't mind.'

She folded her hands in her lap, and fell immediately into a slumber punctuated by the most delicate of snores.

Filomena was chosen to accompany Francesca to her first dancing class. St Christopher's is an extremely ugly wooden building with a corrugated iron roof. The big hall, which echoes dreadfully, has a raised platform at one end. Madame Vera named this platform 'The Stage' and to make it look more stage-like, she hung grey velvet curtains that had seen better days in such a way that they could be pulled across the front of what she called 'The Dancing Space'.

The cloakrooms were painted in a combination of poison-green and a yellowy-beige like uncooked pastry.

'I'll be all right on my own now,' said Francesca. 'You can go.'

'I shall wait for you this time,' said Filomena.

'As it's your first lesson. There are plenty of chairs I can sit on, and I can just as well knit here as at Azalea Avenue.'

Francesca knew better than to argue with Filomena. Of all the Fantoras, Filomena was the one Francesca most resembled, and she knew her grandmother was not easily diverted from her chosen path.

Francesca found a peg, hung up her coat, and began to change into her ballet things. Polly arrived and the two girls began giggling and snorting together at all the things girls giggle and snort about. Soon, the cloakroom was filled with small bodies in tight and shiny pink garments, and a little mountain-range of pink suitcases embossed with ballerinas was beginning to take shape on the floor. In the hall itself, the pianist was warming up. The notes rose and spread into the huge space under the roof, and then fell to the ground again in a shower of trills and cadenzas.

'Where's Dilys?' whispered several girls. 'Has anyone seen Dilys?'

'Who's Dilys?' Francesca wanted to know.

'Ugh!' said Polly. 'She's horrible. Wait till you see her. She's . . .'

At that very moment, the door of the church hall was flung open, and the notorious Dilys appeared. She was a rather square child with yellow plaits and an upturned nose like a pig's.

'Who's that with her?' Francesca whispered. 'Is it her dad?'

'It's her chauffeur,' Polly whispered back. 'Didn't you see his cap? He brings her every week and waits for her in the car park of the supermarket until class is over. She's dead rich. You should see their car. It's black and shiny and just goes on and on. And you can't see into the windows.'

'I expect her dad is a gangster,' said Francesca. 'Ordinary people don't have cars like that.'

'Ssh!' said Polly. 'Don't let her hear you. She'll kill you.'

'I'm not scared of her,' said Francesca. 'So there.'

Still, she decided just to watch Dilys quietly for the moment as it was her very first time at the class. She noticed that Dilys's leotard was pinker and shinier than all the others, her satin shoes looked newer and as for her pink suitcase, the picture of the ballerina on the lid was highlighted with gold paint.

'And look,' she said to Polly, 'she's got frilly bits around the cuffs of her cardigan. I shall call her Frilly Dilys.'

They were laughing so much at this piece of wit that they almost missed the entrance of Madame Vera. She was a stringy person in her late sixties, who made up for her lack of youth and beauty by liberal applications of blusher, lipstick and mauve eyeshadow. False eyelashes as hairy as little tarantulas were stuck to her drooping eyelids. Pearls hung down in ropes nearly to her knees, and made a noise between rustling and clicking every time she moved. As this was a ballet class, Madame Vera moved all the time, and the music of the pearls mingled with the notes spilling out of the piano. To this was added, once the actual dancing had begun, the squeaking of floorboards trodden by twenty pairs of girlish feet.

Filomena said later, 'They should have asked the children to wear ear-muffs. I could hardly hear myself knit. And as for that Madame Vera, she's about as Russian as I am. From her voice, I'd guess Barnsley, but I may be a few miles out.'

'Darlings,' Madame Vera began, in an accent that did indeed seem British in the extreme, 'we have a new pupil with us today, called Francesca Fantora. Francesca, would you like to curtsey for us?'

Francesca obligingly bent her knees and bobbed politely.

'Oh, no, dear, no,' cried Madame Vera, agitating her pearls. 'We shall have to teach you a proper curtsey. Who would like to show Francesca the way we curtsey in this class?'

Everyone in the room was waving frantically, but Frilly Dilys was chosen. She demonstrated the Regulation Curtsey, and Francesca copied her movements exactly.

23

'Lovely! Wonderful! What a quick learner you are, dear!' said Madame Vera. 'I can see you will fit in very well indeed. You are clearly naturally graceful.'

Francesca beamed with pleasure, and failed to notice the expression on Frilly Dilys's face. 'Put out' would be a mild description. 'Dead miffed' was what Polly said later. What was clear was that Francesca had made an enemy.

It did not take more than a few lessons for her to become aware that Frilly Dilys had decided to make her life a misery. She whispered nasty things about Francesca to other girls in the cloakroom, she copied the way Francesca spoke, and she even tried to tempt Polly away with offers of Mars bars and hairslides, but Polly, of course, remained loyal. Francesca was keeping a firm rein on her temper, because she did not want to be expelled from the class, but her patience was wearing dangerously thin.

One day, Madame Vera kept Francesca behind for a few moments of conversation after the rest of the girls had gone to change into their street clothes. By the time she arrived in the cloakroom, almost everyone had gone home, but Polly was standing near the washbasin in tears.

'Polly! Why are you crying? What's happened?'

'It's Frilly Dilys. She's gone and cut every single button off your coat. Look!'

Francesca looked. She turned pale, then scarlet,

then pale again. Her coat was double-breasted. It had ten beautiful brass buttons, and Francesca was extremely proud of them.

'Did you see her do it? Why didn't you hit her or shout at her or pull her hair?'

'I wanted to,' Polly wailed. 'I did. Honestly. I was just going to, only her silly chauffeur was already waiting, so I couldn't. I didn't see her do it. I just saw the buttons in her hand. Oh, your lovely buttons, Francesca! Whatever shall we do? Shall we tell Madame Vera?'

'No,' said Francesca. 'I'm going to do something. All by myself. I shall do it next week. Stop crying. My mum will find other brass buttons.'

'What if they aren't as shiny?'

'They will be even shinier. Don't worry. I don't care about the buttons. I just don't like that Frilly Dilys's horribleness. I never did anything to her.'

'But you dance better, and Madame Vera is always saying so. Frilly Dilys used to be her pet till you came. She can't bear to be second best.'

Francesca said, 'But she's about twentieth best. Lots of other people are better than her.'

'Yes,' Polly explained, 'but Madame Vera can boast and boast that Frilly Dilys comes to her for ballet lessons. The shiny car looks very posh outside the church hall each week. If Frilly Dilys got into a huff and left, then she wouldn't be able to show off about the grand families who send their children to her dancing school. So she's got to favour her.'

'Well, all right,' said Francesca, 'but that still doesn't mean Frilly Dilys can go cutting buttons off other people's coats.' A thought occurred to her. 'She must have been planning it. She must have brought the scissors on purpose.'

'What'll you do?' Polly asked. 'To pay her back?'

'You'll see,' said Francesca. 'Wait till next week.'

The following week, Francesca wore her grubby old anorak to dancing class. Frilly Dilys arrived a little late, as usual.

'She's always a little late,' Francesca whispered to Polly in the cloakroom. 'She has to make sure that everyone's here to be her audience.

Francesca watched carefully as Frilly Dilys took off her street clothes and hung them up. An old-looking yellow plastic mackintosh, a green and black tartan skirt, and a green sweatshirt. Francesca was relieved. If Frilly Dilys's clothes had been too grand, she would have had to delay her revenge. She didn't want anyone saying she had actually spoiled anything.

The girls were called into the hall. Feet squeaked on the floorboards as usual, the music rose into the roof, Madame Vera's pearls rattled and whispered rhythmically.

'Let us start,' said Madame Vera, 'by going through our positions, girls.' She clapped her

26

hands. 'First position!' she trilled, and every foot shuffled into what it considered to be the right place. The lesson had begun.

Twenty minutes before the end of the class, Francesca put her hand up.

'Please, Madame Vera, may I be excused?'

The pearls fell silent for a moment. Madame Vera frowned.

'Yes, Francesca, certainly,' she said, 'but please be quick. Our pliés are in need of some attention. You know that I am Particular about Pliés!'

Francesca ran from the room and the piano began tinkling again. Madame Vera was so involved in the finer points of the plié that she didn't notice how long Francesca was taking. No one noticed except Polly. She was watching the hands of the clock go round. The minutes passed. Where was Francesca? At one point, Polly could have sworn she heard thunder. She looked out of the window. The sky was clear. How very strange, she thought. After fifteen minutes, she was just about to ask permission to go and look for her friend when Francesca came in, smiling sweetly.

'Aha, there you are, dear,' Madame Vera smiled. 'Come along quickly now. I have finished being Particular about Pliés. I am now being Dictatorial about Demi-pliés!' She waited a second or two for the girls to laugh at this witticism, but no one did. Everyone had heard Madame Vera's witticisms many times before.

27

Francesca applied herself diligently to the rest of the afternoon's exercises, and then the class was over. Frilly Dilys sailed into the cloakroom first.

'I must be quick tonight,' Francesca heard her saying to one of her friends. 'Smithers is driving me straight to Veronica's house for tea.'

Francesca smiled as Frilly Dilys disappeared into the cloakroom.

'Wait,' she said to Polly. 'Wait a second and listen carefully.'

Listening carefully was unnecessary. One would have needed to be either stone deaf or in the next street not to hear the shrieks and screams that sliced the air. Francesca and Polly both covered their ears. The shrieking subsided a little after a few seconds and gave way to noisy sobbing. Madame Vera hurried from the hall and pushed her way through the small crowd of girls who had gathered in the door of the cloakroom.

'Now, now,' she said, 'what's this? Oh, Dilys dear, what's happened?'

She went over to where Frilly Dilys was standing, quite unable to speak. Madame Vera looked and saw at once what was wrong. Every single garment that had been hanging on Frilly Dilys's peg was soaked through as though an enormous bucket of water had been tipped over them from the general direction of the ceiling.

'Why!' said Madame Vera, 'your clothes are all

wet! Now how on earth could that have happened? And where is that wind coming from? Oh, it's stopped. Thank goodness for that ... are those hailstones I can see over there? How did hailstones get into this cloakroom? Has it been hailing outside? Perhaps there's a leak ...' She looked hopefully up at the perfectly dry ceiling. 'No, well ...' She frowned. 'This is a mystery, I must say. Have all the taps in those sinks been turned off?'

The sinks were dry and so was the floor beneath them.

'Oh, dear,' Madame Vera was at a loss. 'I'm sure I don't know what can have happened, but I'll have a word with Bill, the caretaker. Now come along, Dilys, dry your eyes, dear. You're just adding to the general wetness.'

Madame Vera tried a light-hearted laugh, but it came out sounding as though she were being strangled. Dilys took everything off her peg, grabbed the handle of her pink suitcase (which looked gratifyingly damp to Francesca ... maybe the gold paint would run) and dripped off down the corridor to where her long, shiny car was waiting outside. When she'd left, the cloakroom returned to normal, although everyone was chattering loudly about what had happened. Madame Vera removed her pearls, put them in her handbag and went off in search of a mop.

'Frilly Dilys is going to drip all over that car,' said Polly, pulling her jumper over her head.

'I know,' said Francesca, 'but it'll soon dry. That hailstorm was a bit of a mistake, and then when I did get it right there wasn't as much rain as I thought there would be.'

'Rain?'

'Yes,' said Francesca rather smugly. 'I made a little raincloud. Just a tiny one, to sit over Frilly Dilys's things and get them wet. It had to be quite little because I didn't want the rain to get on anyone else's clothes, but it did look such a nice fat purply sort of cloud that I thought everything would be even wetter. I wanted a small puddle on the floor.'

'I didn't know you could do that,' Polly said. 'I thought you had to do all your weather things outside.'

'Oh, no,' Francesca put her ballet shoes into her suitcase. 'Doing little bits of weather inside is easy. It's how I started. I only went on to bigger outside things a couple of years ago.'

'Gosh!' said Polly. 'That's amazing. Can you do something to show me?'

Francesca sighed. 'People always want to see,' she said. 'It gets boring. Still, as it's you.'

She waved her fingers half-heartedly above her head and an icicle began to form, hanging down from the end of the coathanger someone had left on her peg.

'There,' she said. 'Now hurry up and finish changing. We've got to get home.'

'Goodness,' said Polly. 'That's lovely. Can I touch it? Can I snap it off and bring it with us?'

'I wouldn't,' said Francesca. 'It'll make you all wet when it melts and you wouldn't want to go home looking like Frilly Dilys, would you?'

Polly giggled as she threw the icicle into one of the sinks, and together they went to find Filomena who had come to collect them.

The Dancing Display

In March, after Francesca had been going to classes for nearly two months, our mealtimes began to be filled with the Dancing Display Saga. First of all, Francesca objected strongly to the dance that had been chosen for her class.

'Everyone else's dance is nicer,' she grumbled. 'Some people are doing the Sailors' Hornpipe, and the big girls are doing a proper dance in real tutus to some *Swan Lake* music, and all we're doing is *Mary, Mary, quite contrary.*'

'I expect it'll be all right,' said Auntie Varvara soothingly, 'on the night. Are you Mary Mary?'

'No,' said Francesca. 'Polly's a Silver Bell, and I'm a Cockle Shell. I have to wear this ridiculous pink thing on my head.'

'Well,' said Rosie, 'never mind. I'm sure you'll look lovely, dear.'

'They could have made us Pretty Maids all in a Row. Ugly Frilly Dilys is Mary Mary. That's really stupid. She's going to be terrible.'

'Why did Madame Vera choose her?' asked Bianca.

'Polly and I think it's because her dad's a gangster. We think it's because he knows some dreadful secret about Madame Vera, and if she doesn't put his daughter in the main part, then he'll tell everyone.'

'I know her awful secret,' said Filomena. 'She comes from Barnsley.'

Everyone laughed and at last we calmed Francesca down.

Rehearsals began. Auntie Varvara, who had done Home Dressmaking at Evening Class three years ago, said that she would make the pinkish silky tunic that Madame Vera had decided was what every Cockle Shell should wear. Francesca practised her steps. Polly practised hers. The day of the dancing display was coming closer. When it actually arrived, Francesca was so excited that she insisted on being the first person to get to the secondary school Madame Vera was using as a theatre.

Rosie took her in the car, and Bianca went with her to keep her company.

'I'll drop you girls off, and come back later,' Rosie said. 'We've all still got to get dressed, so we'll see you at six-thirty. I shall have my work cut out getting Filomena out of her tracksuit.'

Very soon, the dressing room was crowded with Silver Bells, Cockle Shells and Pretty Maids, not to mention Sailors and Swans of all shapes and sizes. Then, just as Polly was beginning to think *she* might be chosen to stand in for her, Frilly Dilys arrived at last.

Her first action was to spot a place she fancied at the mirror, and then push aside everyone else's make-up, combs and brushes to make room for her own. Then she pushed all the costumes on the costume rail to one side and hung up her ballooning and billowy blue skirt.

'She's just as horrible,' Bianca whispered to Francesca, 'as you said she was.'

'Horribler,' Francesca said, trying to fix her rigid pink shell-thingie, as she called it, on to her head like a gigantic pink snail.

'I'm going to sit down now,' Bianca said. 'Good luck. I bet it'll be lovely.'

It wasn't lovely. It was about as far from lovely as a dance could be. Had you been in the audience, you would not have realized that any choreography had taken place at all. To be sure, the Silver Bells, Cockle Shells and Pretty Maids tried to go through their pre-arranged paces as decreed by Madame Vera, but Frilly Dilys, dazzled by the bright lights, decided to do, as they say, her own thing. This mainly involved galumphing around the stage, more or less in time to the music. When she did not galumph, Frilly Dilys careered, and when that became tiresome, she took to whirling. Madame Vera stood in the wings, she and her pearls together frozen into silent horror.

In the audience, Eddie whispered to Rosie, 'Is that what's meant to be happening?'

Rosie shook her head, and Auntie Varvara, who knew about matters balletic, winced and winced again.

'I'm never going to be able to take a proper photograph of Francesca in her costume at this rate,' said Eddie. He had brought his camera, and was all ready to take artistic shots of Francesca's dancing début.

Filomena whispered to Bianca, 'I should have known. I've been doing slip stitches all afternoon, in a very feverish shade of orange. That always means things getting out of control.'

'It's not fair,' said Marco. 'You can't see any of the others. I can hardly see Francesca.'

'There she is,' said Bianca. 'She looks surprisingly happy. Can you see that sunflower, painted on the screen thing, over there?'

Marco looked. Sure enough, there was a tiny piece of scenery right at the back of the stage. It was painted to look like a garden, complete with there or four charmingly fuzzy-looking bees. One should not, of course, blame the painters of the scenery for what happened. They were not to know that Bianca would be tampering with their handiwork. The galumphing continued. It was so loud that only Marco noticed the buzzing at first.

'The bees have come to life, Bianca!' he whispered. 'Is that you?'

'Who else could it be?' Bianca answered.

'You don't know Frilly Dilys is afraid of bees.'

'Bet she is, though,' Bianca smiled.

She was.

Later, no one could agree about exactly what happened. Which came first, the bees or the wind? Opinion is divided. Perhaps (and this, as a Narrator, is the version I favour) three things happened at once:

1) The dance came to an end and the girls lined up at the front of the stage to take their bow, with Francesca standing on Frilly Dily's left.

2) Four bees arrived simultaneously in the neighbourhood of Frilly Dilys.

3) A little wind of about Force 6 whipped up from the footlights region and ran to hide in Frilly Dilys's ballooning, billowy blue skirt.

The result of all this was:

a) Frilly Dilys's skirt blew up over her head, covering her face.

b) Frilly Dilys was stung on the arm by a fuzzy little bee.

c) The applause was deafening.

Later, as the girls were changing into their ordinary clothes, Francesca spoke to Dilys.

'That was me,' she said. 'I made the wind blow, the one that lifted your skirt over your head.' She giggled. 'And my sister brought those bees to life. I bet you didn't know she could do that!'

'I don't believe you . . . ' said Dilys. 'That was an accident.'

'Would you like me to show you?' Francesca smiled. 'Look at that face powder . . . you really ought to keep things like that covered up with me around, you know.'

She waved her fingers over Dilys's open box of powder and a sprightly little breeze blew up.

'I can make it stronger if you like,' said Francesca. 'I can make it blow that stuff all over your frock.'

'No,' said Dilys. 'I believe you now. Do stop. Please.'

'OK.' said Francesca. 'I will. I'm going home now.'

Francesca stalked out, leaving the the other girls staring after her.

I am looking again at one of the photographs Eddie took on that occasion. Francesca likes it so much that she made him enlarge it and put it on the Family Wall. It shows her looking charming in her Cockle Shell outfit, and looking happy, too. She is smiling with what one can only call 'glee'. Beside her is a creature, a shape covered in blue silk. All you can see of this person is chubby legs in lace-trimmed pantaloons. It is Frilly Dilys. Eddie refused to make copies of the photograph for Francesca to distribute to others in her dancing class.

'Frilly Dilys has been punished enough,' he said.

Still, Francesca continues to invite friends into the house all the time, so of course, everyone has seen it.

Frilly Dilys is very polite to Francesca these days. She has even invited her for a ride in the shiny car.

I have noticed an interesting fact about photographs in general and some of these photographs in particular. It is this: whoever is behind the camera decides what is to be in the snapshot, presses the button and eventually a picture appears. This picture, however, does not tell the whole story. There are often other fascinating things happening, as it were, outside the frame. I am reminded of this fact by two small photos (one of Rosie and one of Filomena) which hardly anyone ever sees except me, because they have been placed very low on the wall. I suspect this is because they are not especially flattering. Their tininess is the only thing in their favour. They were taken in what Rosie calls 'one of those dreadful booths which make everyone look like a criminal.' They have been placed on the Family Wall to remind Rosie and Filomena of a day that had significance in their lives. By an extraordinary coincidence, the photographs were taken on the very same day, and it is one that I remember as though it were yesterday. I could see at breakfast that it was going to be busy. Rosie had to attend an interview for the job she had seen advertised in the newspaper. The Barton Bridge College of Further Education was looking for someone willing to put on an imaginative cookery course, which would attract a lot of students.

'Imaginative cookery,' Rosie had said, 'is just what I'm good at.'

She had at once applied for the position, and now here she was, on her way to an interview. Unfortunately, Otter Street Primary School was having what was known as an Occasional Day, and although Bianca, Marco and Francesca were delighted at the unexpected holiday, the grown-ups were less enthusiastic.

'Typical,' said Rosie. 'They always manage to choose the least convenient day. I know the school gave us a couple of weeks' notice, but I have to say the whole matter had slipped my mind. I wouldn't care, only I have to be at the

College at eleven o'clock and they're keeping us the whole afternoon.'

'I'll go with Dad,' said Marco, 'and help him in the shop.'

Eddie munched silently on his toast, thinking of how, last holidays, a customer called Mrs Cartwright had fainted at the sight of three apples being juggled by an invisible Marco.

'All right,' he said at last, 'only I want to be able to see you at all times. Understood?'

Marco nodded.

'That still leaves the girls,' said Rosie.

'May we go to the dressmaker with Auntie Varvara?' Bianca asked.

'Oh no, dear, not today,' said Auntie Varvara quickly. 'I want as few people as possible to see the Dress before the wedding.'

Rosie sniffed a little at this. What she didn't know was that Auntie Varvara's dressmaker, Madame Liliane, who was a dumpy, walnut-faced crone from somewhere exotic that no one had ever quite located exactly, was also an Amateur Clairvoyante, and that Auntie Varvara was given to sitting with her for ages after each fitting, peering at the tea leaves in the bottoms of cups, and laying out pack after pack of slightly grubby playing cards in order to discover what the future held for herself and Remo.

Filomena solved the problem of what was to be done with Bianca and Francesca.

'I shall take the girls to the swimming pool,' she announced. 'There have been distinct signs of water in the knitting: blue silky yarn, chevrons that look like nothing so much as waves, and also . . . well, never mind that . . . I'm sure that's not so important. Water is dominant today. I think we should go to Barton Tub.'

The girls began to jump up and down and a Sugar Puff or two flew through the air and provided some amusement for Monkey and Leopard, who were cavorting about on the top shelf of the dresser.

'There's a huge slide there that goes round and round,' said Bianca, 'and you end up in the water with the most enormous splash.'

Filomena nodded. 'That explains all those long, slinky cables that have been popping up in the knitting. I expect they represent the slide.'

'That's very nice of you, Filomena,' Rosie said. 'Marco, why don't you go with them as well?'

'Yes, why don't you?' said Eddie, looking up hopefully from his newspaper.

'No, thanks,' said Marco. 'I'd rather go with Dad.'

Barton Tub was not Marco's idea of bliss. Water (according to him, and I have to say that I agree with him) had this horrible habit of rushing up your nose, filling your ears, and stinging your eyes. The Big Slide was so terrifying just to think about that he couldn't bear even to glance at it while he was in the pool, and worst of all was the slightly damp, swimming-pooly feeling all over your body all the way home on the bus, with your hair dripping down your neck, and your soggy costume rolled into a soggy bundle and stuffed into a carrier bag that kept banging against your legs as you walked.

Shortly after breakfast then, the Family left the house. First Eddie and Marco drove off in the van, then Auntie Varvara skipped happily up the road, her handbag bulging with love letters from Remo which she was going to read aloud to her luckless dressmaker. Then Filomena and the girls left, and Rosie was the last to go. She was dressed in an unusually smart suit, and she had with her a very large picnic hamper.

'It's not every day,' she said to me, 'that one goes for an interview, Ozzy. I wish to make a good impression.'

I expressed my curiosity about the contents of the hamper. Surely the College would have a canteen where Rosie could have her lunch?

'We have been asked,' she said, 'to cook a demonstration meal. It is part of the interview, you see. They want to know what kind of cookery lessons we will be offering the students, and what sort of course we'll be putting on. I've thought of a very good name for mine already. It's 'Put the Magic into Mealtimes'. It'll be full of new ideas for housewives who are sick to death of all their old recipes.'

43

I purred my approval and good wishes, and Rosie drove off towards the College.

Her adventures there deserve a story to themselves, but before that, I must write about what happened at Barton Tub, and about Auntie Varvara's doings. You will realize at once that all my skills as a Narrator will now be needed. I have to tell two stories at the same time. What about Marco at the shop? I hear you asking. I can answer that question in a trice. Nothing of any interest happened. Marco spent almost the whole day putting various vegetables into carrier bags and that is all.

Lesser Narrators would quail at the thought of what awaits me, but I am looking forward to it. I shall weave my tales together as expertly as I can. Are you ready? Then I'll begin.

Making a Splash

'What on earth,' said Filomena, 'have you got in that rucksack, Bianca?'

'Stuff,' said Bianca, winking secretly at Francesca, who giggled back at her.

The girls and their grandmother were standing at the bus stop, waiting for the bus to take them to Barton Tub. Filomena was carrying a handbag, and she and Francesca each had a carrier bag as well, containing such items as rolled-up towels, swimming costumes and (in Francesca's case) some talcum powder. Bianca, on the other hand, had on her back a little rucksack that bulged alarmingly in ways that suggested Various Other Things were lurking within.

'You haven't got Monkey and Leopard in there, have you?'

Filomena looked worried. The last time Monkey and Leopard had been taken on a bus didn't bear thinking about. They had insisted on sitting on the driver's shoulders. The bus had stopped rather suddenly and all the Fantoras had been asked, politely but firmly, to leave the vehicle.

'No, of course not,' said Bianca. 'They don't like swimming.'

'For which I am deeply grateful,' Filomena said.

The bus arrived and all the other questions Filomena was going to ask Bianca flew out of her head when she discovered she had forgotten her Senior Citizens' Bus Pass.

'Never mind, darling,' said the bus driver, as Filomena was burrowing in her handbag. 'I can see that you qualify. I mean, you're gorgeous and all that, but not that young, know what I mean?'

Filomena handed over the fares.

'How silly I am!' she told the girls. 'I hope this won't cause a problem at Barton Tub. You can usually get a reduction at Leisure Centres. It is one of the good things about growing old.'

There was a dauntingly long queue outside the swimming pool, and Filomena began to look worried all over again.

'It's OK,' said Bianca. 'It's like that because they let people in every two hours. Everyone who is inside comes out and we get our turn. It's ever so quick, honestly. And it's a good idea because it means the pools don't get too crowded.'

Filomena sniffed sceptically. Standing in queues was not her idea of how to spend time. At least here there was something to look at: Barton Tub was the chief attraction of the rather grandly-named Barton Mall: two little rows of ordinary-looking shops.

'There's a café over there,' said Filomena. 'Maybe we'll have a cup of tea after our swim.'

'There's a café inside Barton Tub,' said Francesca. 'It's much nicer. Wait till you see it.'

Just then, the huge glass doors of the Leisure Centre slid open, and the queue began moving rapidly towards the ticket office.

'Nearly there now,' said Bianca. 'I'm longing, longing, longing for you to see it.'

'I've been to more swimming-pools,' said Filomena, 'than you've had hot dinners. It'll take a lot to impress me.'

'Enter! enter! Please to enter, dearest Miss Varvara!'

47

Madame Liliane smiled when she saw who was at her door. Auntie Varvara was a client after her own heart, a client like the ones she used to have in the Old Country, in the days when women had Time and Money and could sit and drink mint tea with her all afternoon as the sun grew lower and lower in the sky and the shadows lengthened. In the Good Old Days, women had nursemaids and chauffeurs to look after them, and cooks to prepare every meal, and could spend hours choosing fabric and coming for fittings, and Madame Liliane was used to stitching delicious little bits of gossip into her conversation, to please her ladies. Nowadays, everything was different. Everyone bought dresses ready-made in big shops where nothing was properly finished, and if they ever did find her and use her considerable skills, it was all rush-hurry, rush-hurry, in for five minutes for a fitting, and then off to unfreeze a block of something tasteless, or collect children from school, or take them somewhere in the car. Madame Liliane thought that the old ways were dead until she met Varvara Fantora.

At first, it is true, Madame Liliane did not believe everything she was told.

'I don't tell everyone,' Auntie Varvara had whispered the first time she had come for a consultation, 'but I think it important that you should know. I am a vampire and my fiancé comes from a long line of Italian werewolves.'

Madame Liliane said nothing, so Auntie Varvara continued, 'A very distinguished and aristocratic family of Italian werewolves.'

'Of course,' Madame Liliane said. 'I understand perfectly.'

'My mother doesn't like us to tell just anyone, you know. She says it's vulgar to flaunt gifts like that at people. But I think the relationship between a dressmaker and her client is a very personal one, and I don't think we should keep things from one another, don't you agree?'

Madame Liliane nodded. Here, she was thinking, is a talkative woman who will be happy to spend an hour or two on each fitting. If she wishes to call herself a vampire and have fantasies about werewolves, it's none of my business.

In fact, 'I have certain powers of my own,' she said, looking down modestly at her hands.

'Oh, I know!' Auntie Varvara cried. 'Everyone says your dresses are the purest magic.'

'Not the dresses,' said Madame Liliane. 'Something else. I can see into the future.'

Madame Liliane had hoped for a more enthusiastic reaction. How was she to know that this vampire-person had a mother who could read the future from her knitting? Of all the peculiar things Madame Liliane had seen in her long life, this was the strangest.

Still, all had turned out most satisfactorily. It seemed that the mother was not allowed to hear

49

the love-letters coming from this Remo, so Madame Liliane had devised a form of fortune-telling that suited both herself and Auntie Varvara perfectly. Auntie Varvara would read bits of her letters, and then the two ladies would drink tea, and the tea leaves and letters together produced an 'aura' (that was Madame Liliane's word) suitable for the foretelling of the distant future, Auntie Varvara's future after she was married.

'Your mother's knitting,' said Madame Liliane, 'cannot foretell the distant future?'

'Oh no,' said Auntie Varvara, 'just the next few days.'

Madame Liliane folded her arms, satisfied that her magic had triumphed. The fact that she made up every prediction out of her head was neither here nor there. Even if Auntie Varvara had known, she probably wouldn't have minded. She enjoyed the company, the talk, the cosy little room piled high with rolls of material and pattern books, and crowded with cushions and boxes of pins and little knick-knacks, and the fact that she, Auntie Varvara, was the centre of attention.

Now, here she was again for another fitting. She stepped happily into Madame Liliane's flat, and closed the door behind her.

'Told you so!' said Francesca. 'We told you you wouldn't believe your eyes.'

50

'And you were right,' Filomena said. 'I never expected anything like this at all.'

She stared at the huge glass dome of the building, the plants that clung to everything a plant could possibly cling to, the marble walls and floors and (just visible through a glass door) the Jungle Café beside the Main Pool.

'Can you see the lovely yellow chairs?' Bianca said. 'And look at the parrots in the trees. Aren't they sweet?'

'They're not real, are they?' Filomena asked.

'They could be,' Bianca said. 'If you like.'

'I do *not* like,' Filomena said. 'On no account are you to bring those parrots to life. That's all we need.'

The queue came nearer and nearer to the ticket office. Brightly-coloured posters stuck to a big blackboard announced Barton Tub's other attractions: 'Jacuzzi, sauna, aerobics classes, giant trampoline'.

'Look, girls,' said Filomena. 'Look at that! A giant trampoline. I shall certainly have a go on that.'

At the window of the ticket office, she said, 'One Senior Citizen and two children, please.'

'Three pounds,' said the young person at the till.

'Does that include the Giant Trampoline?' Filomena asked.

'No, you need a Barton Tub Leisure Pass for that.'

'Then please may I have one of those?'

'They're five pounds. And you need a photograph. Passport-sized.

'I haven't got one,' said Filomena, 'and I do want to use the Giant Trampoline today. Can't you make an exception? Just this once?'

'No, sorry,' said the young person. 'But you can get one done in the photo booth in the Mall and then come back here.'

Filomena paid three pounds and took her three tickets. She said to Bianca, 'Now I'm not going to be long, and you're both sensible girls and know how to swim, so I'll let you go into the pool without me, and I'll hurry and get my photo taken and collect my Leisure Pass and come and join you. Will you be all right on your own?'

'Of course we will,' said Bianca.

Filomena was so preoccupied with visions of herself on a Giant Trampoline that she missed the wicked gleam in Bianca's eyes.

Filomena hurried out into the Mall and the two girls made their way to the changing room.

'Are you sure,' said Francesca, 'that we're allowed to bring bath toys into the pool?'

'I've never seen any notices saying we can't,' said Bianca, 'and in any case, we're only going to put them in the Baby Pool.'

When she and Francesca had changed into their swimming-costumes, they tiptoed through the foot-bath and into the pool area.

'There's the slide,' said Francesca. 'Look!'

The noise of rushing water filled the air, so that Francesca had to shout to make herself heard. The girls had their arms full of bath toys: two fish made of orange plastic, a little blue and white boat with a green chimney, and a family of rubber ducks – mother and four little ducklings, with bright eyes and shiny red beaks. No one noticed the girls at first, or paid any attention to what they were carrying. It was hard to believe that in a matter of moments, Barton Tub would be learning what the words Total Chaos meant.

Auntie Varvara was in the middle of reading her fourth love-letter.

'And then he says, "Bellissima Varvara, how I long for June when we shall be together! The preparations my mother and sister are making for their wedding outfits are the talk of the town. Fabrics are flown in for inspection, designers submit drawings every day, the bank vault has been cleared of the family jewels which have lain there for years and three jewellers have taken up residence in one of the rooms we hardly use and are working day and night to clean each gemstone till it shines as brightly as your eyes, cara mia."'

Auntie Varvara sighed blissfully and took another sip of tea.

'They are not poor, your relations-in-law to be,' Madame Liliane nodded wisely.

'Oh no,' said Auntie Varvara.'Quite the reverse. Palazzos and villas and things all over the place. Which is fortunate because I can't think what Remo would do if he had to work for a living!' She chuckled affectionately. 'Such a dreamer! Such a romantic! I can't wait for him to see me in my dress . . . it's going to be beautiful.'

'I hope you haven't told anyone,' Madame Liliane frowned.

'Not a soul,' Auntie Varvara smiled. 'No one has the least idea of what it will be like. Even my mother can't guess from her knitting. All she knows is that the colours are becoming more and more vibrant. It's the excitement about the wedding, she says.'

'Let us see,' said Madame Liliane, 'what is in the leaves today.'

Two heads bent low over the teacups.

'Towers,' said Madame Liliane firmly. 'Very tall square ones . . . possibly skyscrapers.'

'A honeymoon in New York!' Auntie Varvara clapped her hands. 'Oh, I do hope that's what it means! Remo loves America with a passion.'

'Let us hope that is what they mean, then,' said Madame Liliane. 'Do help yourself to another biscuit.'

The plate had been left on the table across the room from where the two women were sitting. Auntie Varvara looked at it for some moments and nodded. The plate rose gently, smoothly into the air and landed silently beside her teacup. The biscuits on it had not moved at all. Madame Liliane turned a little pale.

'Did . . . you do that?'

'Bring the plate over? Oh, yes. Nothing to it at all. I've always been able to move things. Look, I'll fetch the scissors . . .'

While Madame Liliane's mouth fell open in amazement, her dressmaking scissors soared through the air towards her hand with all the grace of a long-legged silver bird. Madame Liliane gulped. Perhaps she would have to reconsider her views about vampires and werewolves.

Bianca and Francesca were splashing around in the Baby Pool with their bath toys bobbing about harmlessly beside them. Barton Tub was full. Happy shouts and laughter, the general splashings and gurglings one would expect to hear in any swimming pool swelled and filled the enormous glass dome. Those who were hurtling down the Big Slide shrieked with excitement or terror or both together. The life guards in their pink track-suits walked around the edge of the pool making sure that no one was in danger. It was a swimming session like any other. Then, Bianca brought to life her two plastic fish, the little steamboat and the family of ducks. Who could have foreseen that seven little creatures could wreak such havoc?

There are times (and this is one of them) when I wish I were a camera. I would have loved to be up in the glass dome of Barton Tub, able to show in one enormous photograph everything that was happening in the pool below. But I am not a camera, and therefore I shall have to describe, one after another, several separate chains of events *which were all going on at the same time*. Seven small creatures came to life, and all manner of disasters followed.

The first little fish surprised an elderly lady paddling near the shallow end by jumping down the front of her costume. The lady promptly fainted, was dragged out of the pool by two lifeguards, one of whom overbalanced and tumbled into the pool on top of an elderly gentleman who had been silly enough to go swimming with his false hairpiece on. This hairpiece fell into the water and frightened two little girls as it went floating past them. They screamed and rushed out of the pool, colliding with a rather wobbly lady who landed heavily on her bottom in a gigantic tub of ferns, which overturned, causing black potting compost to be spread over a wide area.

The second little fish swam into the main pool and was captured by a boy who intended to smuggle it out of the pool in the pocket of his swimming trunks. Unfortunately, he tried to put the fish into the pocket just in that part of the water where two fast-moving currents met, and his trunks were pulled right off. As he dived under water to pull them up, the fish escaped and went leaping about in the rushing water. Lots of people saw it and decided to chase it, so there were groups of screaming children and adults all thrashing about in the deep end. A particularly high wave (someone had turned on the wave machine!) threw the fish out of the water and it landed in a glass of lemonade on one of the tables in the poolside café. The child whose lemonade it was tossed the fish back into the water, and of course, the lemonade along with it. The child's mother pulled the child away from the edge and bumped into a table, which fell over, spilling chips and sausages on to the floor. One sausage rolled into the pool, and of course, people started chasing it.

The steamboat stayed in the Baby Pool. Two toddlers became particularly fond of the way it chugged along and a fight over ownership broke out. Mothers ran to the scene, tears flowed, a third child decided *she* wanted the little boat and she simply snatched it and clasped it to her chest and began to climb up the steps to the changing room.

Meanwhile, Mother Duck was waddling calmly along with three pink-clad lifeguards tiptoeing behind her, trying to catch her. People kept getting in the way, or else they decided to join the hunt and so in a few moments there was a long line of assorted bathers and spectators snaking round the tiled edge of the pool.

Two of the ducklings had found the footbath, and many large children had gathered to watch their antics. As this was also the way into the changing-rooms, anyone wanting to go home had to fight a way through the crowd, and risk having their toes playfully nipped by the fluffy little creatures.

The last two ducklings were creating a sensation in the café. Everyone tried to tempt them with crumbs from their sesame buns. People suddenly wanted nothing so much as a duckling to come and sit with them at their table, so they started clicking their fingers and making the silly sorts of 'tsk,tsk'-ing sounds they usually reserved for puppies and kittens.

Have I conveyed the scene to you? Can you hear the wailing, crying, splashing, snorting, tsking, clucking, chugging, shouting and roaring? Can you see dozens ... no, scores ... of people dashing, pulling, chasing, sliding, swimming, falling, tiptoeing round and round in different directions? Can you imagine water, earth, plants, people, chairs, tables, food and drink all tossed and scattered and broken and mixed up together? Then you have some notion of what it was like in Barton Tub that day.

It was when the chaos was at its height that

Filomena returned to the pool, ready to hand in her photograph and collect her Leisure Pass. She was not in the best of tempers. She was muttering to herself about Photo Booths and the way, no matter how hard you tried, the seat was never the right height, and you always ended up looking either as if you were fighting to be seen over a high wall, or as if your head was being squashed against the ceiling. The flash was too bright and shone on your glasses, the light drained your face of all colour and it was no wonder, thought Filomena, that a person came out looking bewildered and stupid and always a little grey.

'I'm afraid we're not issuing any more Leisure Passes today,' said the young person at the till. 'There's been a bit of a crisis, you see.'

Filomena saw. Filomena was good at seeing. It was her special talent. Just this morning she had been knitting some wool which had made her very nervous, because, as she put it, 'With wool like that, there's no telling *what* might happen.'

It was one of those blends of five different colours, with blobs and lumps and irregularities spun into it, and Filomena knew that it meant disorder of some kind.

'I should have been prepared,' she said to herself. 'And I should never have left Bianca and Francesca on their own. I was carried away by dreams of a Giant Trampoline, and I will never forgive myself if anything has happened to my granddaughters.'

She found the girls in the changing-room, drying themselves.

'Thank goodness you're all right,' she cried. 'Whatever has been going on?'

'I'm not quite sure,' said Bianca. 'Someone fainted . . . then a boy's swimming-trunks came off . . . and people started being silly. It's all right now, though.'

Filomena glanced through the glass wall. Things were quieter. In fact, if it were not for the furniture upside down in the café, and a couple of ferns and some plastic mugs still in the water, Barton Tub would have looked almost normal. One of the lifeguards had brought a huge net and was collecting everything that had fallen into the pool. Bianca waited until Filomena was busy drying Francesca's hair, and then she went up to him.

'Excuse me,' she said. 'I've left something behind. It's my bath toys. I was too frightened to get them before when it was all noisy.'

'Are these them?' said the lifeguard. 'You look a bit big for things like this, if you ask me.'

'They belong to my little sister,' said Bianca, opening her rucksack. 'We thought they were lost.'

'Shouldn't be allowed,' spluttered the lifeguard. 'Probably isn't allowed.'

'I'll tell my sister,' said Bianca sweetly, 'not to bring her bath toys to Barton Tub again.'

'Right,' said the lifeguard. 'You do that,'

He thought about his lunch. He needed it after what had gone on this morning. He wasn't himself. The plastic fish he'd just put into that girl's rucksack looked just like the one that had jumped into the old lady's costume, earlier on. He wasn't going to say a word, though. He certainly didn't want anyone thinking he was losing his grip, oh no indeed.

On the bus on the way home, Francesca said, 'Did you get your Leisure Pass, Filomena?'

Filomena said, 'No. I got four dreadful photographs of myself instead, and one of them I shall put on the Family Wall to be a lesson to me in the future. I must pay closer attention to the wool and to my duty and not be led astray by Giant Trampolines.'

'You can get yourself a Leisure Pass next time we go,' said Bianca.

'I have every intention of doing so,' said Filomena, 'but I shall visit Barton Tub in future when you young ladies are safely at your desks at school.'

Auntie Varvara arrived back from Madame Liliane's house full of excitement.

'My dress will be divine, Ozzy,' she told me. 'It will be like no other wedding dress you've ever seen.'

61

I purred obligingly, and omitted to tell Auntie Varvara that I had seen hardly any wedding dresses to speak of. I understood what she was trying to tell me. Hers was going to be a little out of the ordinary.

'I shall have to get Eddie to grow me some special lilies. I need deep, deep turquoise. I wonder whether . . . ' she murmured and made a note in a small notebook she had taken to carrying about with her at all times, because, as she put it, 'You never know when something may strike you.'

I myself rely on the Notebook of Memory, but I can see why someone as scatterbrained as Auntie Varvara may need to write down every stray thought.

Speaking of Memory reminds me: do you remember my photograph and the small mystery I have woven round it? It was on the evening of the Occasional Day that my adventures took a small step forward. Marco and Bianca began to look at me in a deliberate and meaningful way and say such things to one another as, 'I think he looks more dignified sitting up' or, 'We should get him when he's not looking out of the window' or, 'What about putting him on someone's lap? Francesca's maybe. He'd look cute.' I shuddered to hear myself being described as 'cute' but could not imagine why Bianca and Marco should be so interested in my appearance. The mystery deepens . . .

Rosie's Magical Menu

Now, as I promised, I am turning my attention to Rosie. The day of the Barton Tub Ballyhoo was a momentous one for her also. I would ask my readers to think themselves back to the morning of that day, and to imagine Rosie setting off for her first job interview in years. On her way to the College, although she was understandably a little nervous, she thought she knew what to expect. There would be a table, with clever-looking people sitting behind it, and these clever-looking people would ask difficult questions in a stiff and formal way. It would be a little like being seen by the headteacher.

How wrong I was! she thought, as she opened her hamper and began to take out her ingredients. A very toothy young lady called Janet had spoken to all the interviewees.

'We're terribly informal here,' she beamed. 'We're going to leave all of you to cook your individual dishes and then after lunch (which we shall all eat together) you will be seen one by one, and before you go home, we will let you know which one of you has been successful.'

She had then taken Rosie and the three other candidates who wanted the job into the College kitchen.

Rosie studied her fellow competitors as she chopped onions. She had decided before leaving home that she should try to succeed purely on the merit of her chosen dish, which she called Rainbow Rice, and not use any magic powers at all to help herself, but one glance at her companions had changed her mind.

'I'm Priscilla Plumtree,' said a tall and willowy red-headed lady with long, purple nails, who, Rosie noticed, did not even bother to wash her hands before starting to cook.

'Delighted to meet you,' said a leathery-looking elderly man in rather grubby tweeds. 'I'm Malcolm

Summers, and this is exactly what I'm used to. I had twenty-five years in the Prison Service, you know, before I retired. Early retirement, of course,' he added. 'Ha! Ha!'

Rosie thought being in prison must be quite dreadful enough without having to eat food cooked by Malcolm, but she smiled and said nothing. Now she could see from across the room that Malcolm's stew was indeed going to turn out watery and tasteless. She shuddered.

The last competitor, who was making meringues that looked light enough to float off the plate by themselves, was quite different.

'I'm Renee,' she announced in a little girl's voice, 'and I'm not sure if I want this job or not, really. I mean, I really want something that's more than one morning a week, but I suppose this'll be better than nothing.'

Rosie frowned. What a trio, she thought. One was unhygienic, another made dreadfully tasteless food, and a third was not fully committed to the work. It would be a sin and a shame to let any one of them loose on the hapless students of the College, who were, after all, paying good money for their classes. There was no other alternative. She would have to do something really spectacular. Rainbow Rice, she thought. Red, green and yellow peppers won't be nearly enough. I shall have to make it in proper rainbow colours ... oh, dear! For a moment she was so deep in thought that she absent-mindedly allowed a knife to slip out of a drawer and begin, all by itself, to chop a couple of onions that were lying on the work surface. When the knife had done its work, a small white shower of onion pieces rose like a fountain, and after describing a graceful curve, settled into a conveniently-placed frying pan with a deliciously satisfying sizzle. Mr Summers, who saw this happening, trembled to think he might be losing his grip on reality, and took another sip from a small bottle hidden in his briefcase. Rosie had come to a decision. It's not very fair, she said to herself, and I wouldn't do it if I didn't truly think I was the best candidate for the job, but whatever's the point of having magic powers, if you don't use them? She sighed and turned her attention to the production of indigo, blue and violet vegetables.

'Well, now,' said Janet, smiling at Rosie and the three other interviewees, 'this looks like a lunch fit for a queen . . . or even for a panel of hungry interviewers!'

Rosie, Priscilla, Malcolm and Renee smiled weakly at what they thought was meant to be a joke.

Everyone sat down at the table and Janet dished out the first course from the enormous soup tureen.

'This,' she announced, 'is Priscilla's Watercress and Stilton soup.'

Spoons were dipped, the soup was sipped and

sipped again. Most of the eaters stopped there, although Rosie noticed that Janet and the Panel suffered through a few more spoonfuls, before giving up the struggle.

'I can't understand it,' Priscilla was red in the face. 'This soup is sweet, and it isn't supposed to be sweet. It's never been sweet before. I suppose I must have been nervous and added sugar instead of salt! How dreadfully careless of me!'

'It could happen to anyone,' said Janet. 'Accidents happen in every kitchen. We understand perfectly.'

The stew arrived. It was as watery and tasteless as Rosie had feared it would be.

'Mmm,' said Janet, trying to suck a strand of meat from between two teeth. 'Very . . . nourishing,' she added, desperately spearing a carrot. 'I must have some of Rosie's Rainbow Rice now.'

There was silence around the table as everyone ate the rice. Rosie knew her rice tasted wonderful, and she could see that it looked astonishing, but just to make sure, she had at the very last moment, added a pinch of something special, something magical which made everyone at the table feel blissfully contented.

'Delicious!' Janet breathed, her eyes shining. 'Wherever did you find all these rainbow-coloured vegetables?'

'Please, please will you tell us the recipe?' pleaded Renee.

'Heaven!' exclaimed Priscilla.

'Absolutely top notch!' said Malcolm, helping himself to seconds.

Renee's meringues were next. Rosie took a bite from one and could hardly believe what she was tasting. The meringues had turned out salty.

'It's almost as though,' Renee said to Priscilla, 'your salt and my sugar had got mixed up.'

'That's probably exactly what happened,' said Janet. 'It's very easily done when there are several people cooking together. Isn't there a saying about too many cooks?'

Rosie sipped her coffee. After all the effort she had put into her rice, Priscilla and Renee had spoiled their own chances all by themselves. Still, indigo mushrooms, blue parsley and violet radishes did look pretty, she had to admit.

'However do you manage the colours?' Janet asked.

'Oh,' said Rosie airily, 'I find that if you speak to vegetables politely, they're most obliging, although I did once meet an aubergine which would *not* take to being striped in yellow and white, however hard I tried. For the most part though, vegetables are willing to try most things.'

There was silence round the table, and then Janet chuckled nervously.

'I can see that Rosie is giving nothing away. Quite right, Rosie. We cooks must guard our precious secrets, must we not?'

'I suppose we must,' said Rosie.

Malcolm, examining a dark-blue mushroom before popping it into his mouth, was heard to mutter darkly about fiendish new advances in food dyes in the United States.

'And so,' said Janet, 'we come to the moment you have all been waiting for. Although of course all four of you are the most excellent cooks, I'm afraid three of you will be going home a little disappointed. We've decided to let Rosie Fantora put on her course, which,' (she consulted a clipboard) 'is going to be called: *Put the Magic into Mealtimes.* Thank you all so much for applying and better luck next time.'

Priscilla, Malcolm and Renee all smiled and shook Rosie's hand and congratulated her. Rosie herself felt so happy that without even thinking about it, she rose several inches into the air. No, no, she told herself, I can't fly about now, not after all that fuss about the coloured vegetables. That would never do. I shall wait till I go home, and then fly back and tell everyone the good news. She forced herself down to the ground again and smiled shyly.

'Thank you,' she said.

After the others had left, Janet took Rosie into an office where she filled in forms and arranged to come in for her first class on the following Thursday.

'You will need,' said Janet, 'a passport photo for your College Identity Card. There's a machine just next to the cafeteria as you leave.'

Of the four photographs of Rosie that came out of the booth, two were unspeakable and had to be instantly destroyed, one was stuck to her Identity Card and covered with plastic and the last was put up on the Family Wall to remind Rosie of one of her more spectacular successes.

As she left the College, she felt the familiar tingling in her feet, and took off spontaneously into the air, rising higher and higher over the trees. She had wafted in the general direction of Azalea Avenue for quite some time before she recalled that her car was still parked in the College car park. She sighed and turned back at once. Three elderly gentlemen who had been to the College to sign up for a class in Home Beer-making saw her drifting down and down from a spot that seemed to be some metres above the tallest tree. Each man thought the same thing to himself: 'I wonder if this Beer-making's a good idea. I'm seeing things now. Better not say anything to the others. They'll think I'm soft in the head.'

So, nobody mentioned it and Rosie arrived at her car and drove sedately all the way home.

Today, Dora Collins has just informed me, is a beautiful day, and yet here I am, still indoors. I have a confession to make about OUTSIDE and it is this. I find it unreliable, and therefore, unless there are persuasive reasons (the Family are lolling about the garden and I do not want to miss anything, let us say) I would rather lie beside the open window in a small square of sunlight than risk unexpected draughts, irritating insects and such minor inconveniences as clouds covering the sun, noisy portable radios and the like. It was not always so. In my younger days I was a Hunter and a Prowler, a Chaser and a Growler. I was the scourge of squirrels, the bane of every butterfly and bird. Not many people know that I have an ear with a scar on it – oh, I am the veteran of many a scrap! But that was all long, long ago, and now what I enjoy are the pleasures of the mind. I love the *look* of the outside, make no mistake. I gaze at the sky through the skylight whenever I go up for a snooze on Auntie Varvara's bed, and wonder at its beauty without having to suffer any of the nasty surprises it sometimes has up its sleeve: rain, wind, snow and so forth.

I am also fond of photographs depicting the Great Outdoors. Here on the Family Wall, for example, is a splendidly breezy picture of Bianca, which was taken on a recent school outing. The whole class went to Yorkshire for a few days, on an Educational Trip. Such things as Rock Formations, Farming and Botany were going to be studied. Orienteering had been mentioned. The children stayed at Henston Hall, a Victorian school which had been converted into a Youth Hostel. Bianca enjoyed herself. You can see it in the photograph. She is grinning widely at the camera. She has a rucksack on over her anorak. The wind is blowing her hair about and behind her the landscape is full of the things the landscape is generally full of: rocks, trees, a smallish mountain in the distance, and an awful lot of sky, dotted about with a few pleasantly puffy clouds. The photograph has in it, though, one rather strange feature. There are two pretty little cats at Bianca's feet. Their fur is white spotted with ginger, and their faces wear a delightfully calm expression. They have very pale green eyes like boiled gooseberries. They do not look like outdoor cats to me. Rather, they're the sort of cats you would find on either side of a fireplace.

While Bianca was away, she sent us all a post-card with a picture of a sheep on it.

'Having a lovely time,' she wrote. 'There are lots of sheep here.'

There was no mention of cats, ginger-spotted or otherwise. I learned what happened later, after Bianca had come home, and this is the story.

Strange Happenings at Henston Hall

Marco and Francesca were helping Bianca with her packing, and I was curled up on the bed, listening to the children talking. Bianca was getting ready for her school trip to Henston Hall in Yorkshire. A sleeping-bag looking like an enormous Swiss Roll was waiting by the door, and her rucksack was filling up nicely.

'What does this mean?' asked Marco, reading

from the list the school had provided, which was headed: *Things to bring with you*. "Teddy Bear or similar." There's nothing similar to a teddy bear. Not that I can think of. What on earth do you need to take a teddy bear for?'

'It's in case people get homesick,' said Bianca. 'Teachers think that having a teddy from home will cheer them up. Or something like a teddy. Some kind of cuddly toy.'

'You're only going for three nights,' said Francesca. 'Why on earth would anyone be homesick?'

'It's the first time some of us have been away from home.'

'If it was me,' said Francesca, 'I'd take Monkey and Leopard.'

'You could take Mandy or Candy,' said Marco. (These were Bianca's dolls who lived in an extremely well-appointed dolls' house beside the chest-of-drawers.) 'Or even Shandy.' (Shandy was their dog.)

'No,' said Bianca. 'They're too noisy. And can you imagine Candy and Mandy enjoying life in a Youth Hostel?' She giggled. Candy and Mandy only ever wore sparkling ballgowns or equally sparkling bikini-sets. Yorkshire was not the place for them. 'I shall take Dodger, because he's an actual teddy bear, not a 'similar' and because he's quite little and will fit in my rucksack.'

So Dodger it was who sped up the motorway

with Bianca and her classmates and found himself
at last on a top bunk in a large room containing
five other bunk-beds, an ancient cupboard and
very little else. Bianca opened the cupboard at
once and looked inside.

'What are you looking for, Bianca?' Jenny
asked.

'Nothing,' said Bianca, 'only I like cupboards
and you never know what someone's left behind
in there.'

'Has anyone left anything?' Jenny peered into
the dark space.

'There's something in that corner, wrapped in
a cloth.'

'Probably a skull,' said Tanya. 'I dare you to
unwrap whatever it is.' She made some ghostly
noises.

'Shut up,' said Bianca. 'You'll have the boys in
here in a minute. Of course I dare open it. It's
not a bit skull-shaped.'

'Perhaps it's a severed hand,' Tanya suggested.
'A withered severed hand.'

As Bianca started unwrapping, it became clear
that there were two objects wound up in the
dusty rags.

Tanya said, 'Two severed hands . . .'

'It's only two china ornaments,' said Bianca.
'So there. They're a bit broken, though.'

She set the two china cats on the windowsill.
One had an ear missing, and the other had a bit

chipped off the end of its paw. The cats were white, speckled with orange blobs.

'They look like book ends,' said Sarah. 'Both sitting up and facing out like that. They're pretty aren't they? It's a shame they're a bit knocked about. They must be quite old, mustn't they?'

'I suppose so,' said Bianca, losing interest. 'Let's unroll our sleeping-bags and then we can go and explore the rest of this place.'

The girls spread out their bedding, laid their rucksacks neatly at the ends of their bunks, and set off.

Henston Hall was a big, echoey sort of place set in one of the rockier parts of the Pennines. Mr and Mrs Page, the old couple who looked after the house, lived in two rooms to the right of the enormous front door. The schools who came to visit Henston Hall brought most of their own food with them, and the teachers and children took turns to cook and wash up, but the Pages made sure that everything went smoothly, and that fresh milk, eggs and bread were available.

'I wouldn't have liked going to school here,' said Sarah. 'Imagine how cold it must have been in the winter!'

'It's not exactly boiling hot now, is it?' said Bianca. 'Never mind, it'll soon be time for supper. I'm longing for it. I'm really hungry.'

Had Bianca known what supper was going to be like, she would not have longed for it. No indeed. She would have bought some more crisps and chocolates at the motorway café and made do with them. The beefburgers were thin and flabby and grey, the chips were thick and flabby and yellow, and the baked beans were a special cheap kind with the sort of sauce that didn't taste right. Most people ate most of what there was because they were hungry, but Bianca left half of hers. For a moment she thought yearningly of Rosie's snowdrifts of mashed potato, of her ice-cream and chocolate sauce. She wouldn't even have said no to one of Auntie Varvara's vegeburgers. Perhaps this was what everyone meant by homesickness. Across the table, Jonathan Baxter, well-known noisemaker and general pain-in-the-neck, was doing disgusting things to his beefburger, but Bianca could see he had no intention of eating it. Quite a few of his chips remained untouched as well. Pudding was stale yellow sponge-cake with greenish icing on it. At the end of the meal, all the children helped with the washing-up and putting away. Bianca and Sarah noticed that there were all sorts of quite edible things in the cupboard.

'Look!' Sarah whispered. 'Biscuits!'

'And cornflakes,' said Bianca. 'I expect they're for breakfast. There's bread and jam as well, look. And some honey.' She was speaking quietly, too. 'I've got a good idea. When everyone's asleep, we can creep down here and have a midnight feast. Just like in those books where they're always doing stuff like that.'

'How will we stay awake?' asked Sarah.

'I won't be able to sleep,' said Bianca. 'I'll be too hungry.'

'So if I do go to sleep, you can wake me up. When do you think it'll be safe?'

'Midnight,' said Bianca. 'If we're going to have a midnight feast, we ought to have it at midnight.'

'Right,' said Sarah. 'Can't wait!'

When midnight came, Bianca was the only person in the room who was still awake. The journey, the meal, the games after supper and the squealing and squeaking and wriggling into sleeping-bags in an unfamiliar place had been too much for most people, and they had fallen fast asleep. Bianca tried to wake Sarah by pushing at her shoulder, but Sarah refused to be woken. She turned over on her tummy and buried her face in the pillow.

'I'll have to go on my own,' Bianca said to Dodger, who had been brought to life because there was no one else to talk to. 'I'm so hungry. I can't sleep for thinking about all those packets of biscuits I saw in the cupboard. Come on, Dodger, you come with me.'

'Must I?' Dodger whispered.

'Yes, you must.' Bianca was quite firm. 'You're supposed to be keeping me company.'

'But I'm scared,' said Dodger.

'What are you scared of? There's nothing to be scared of.'

'I wouldn't be so sure about that,' said Dodger. 'This is a very old building. It's almost sure to be haunted.'

'Haunted?' Bianca's voice quavered slightly.

'Oh, yes,' said Dodger. 'Sure to be. You know, wailing Victorian schoolchildren, evil teachers, sinister caretakers with black eyebrows and scars all over their cheeks.'

'That's nonsense,' said Bianca. 'You're just trying to get out of coming with me because you'd rather go back to sleep. Well, tough luck! You're coming, so there. If you're good, you can have a biscuit.'

Bianca and Dodger crept out of the bunk, tiptoed across the room and went out into the corridor that led from the girls' dormitory across the front hall past the Pages' rooms and down to the kitchen. Thank goodness the corridor lights were on. Everything *did* look different at night. Scarier. Spookier. Bianca didn't believe in any of Dodger's silly tales, but the shadows just over there were very black, and weren't they a strange shape, and wasn't that something moving, fluttering in that corner?

'Stop being so stupid,' she said aloud to herself. 'There's nothing there. Nothing at all.'

She cheered herself up by thinking about biscuits. The kitchen was getting nearer and nearer.

'Almost there, Dodger,' she whispered, and then she heard it. An awful, ghastly, ghostly, heartrending noise, like someone crying and crying and sniffing and trying not to be heard. All the hairs on the back of her neck stood up, stiff with terror.

'It's one of those children,' she said to Dodger. 'The ghost of a child who was at school here years ago ... oh, it's horrible, Dodger. Why are we still standing here? Let's go back. I'm not hungry any more, all of a sudden.'

'That's not a ghost,' said Dodger, sounding very brave. 'That's one of your friends.'

'It can't be,' said Bianca. 'They're all asleep.'

'Not from your room, silly. From the boys' room.'

'How do you know?' Bianca asked.

'I had a look round the door,' said Dodger, 'while you were busy being rooted to the spot with horror. It's that big, red-faced boy with the spiky haircut.'

'Jonathan Baxter? I don't believe you. He never cries. He shouts a lot, though. That's what he's good at.'

'Nevertheless,' said Dodger. 'It's him.'

Bianca walked into the kitchen and sure enough, there was Jonathan, sitting at the big table, holding a chocolate biscuit in one hand and crying as if he never meant to stop.

'What's the matter, Jonathan?' Bianca asked. 'What is it?'

81

Jonathan looked as though he'd been turned into a statue. Bianca Fantora and a walking teddy bear? When he thought of what she would tell her friends about him in the morning, he began to cry louder than ever.

'Stop it,' said Bianca.

She went over to where a roll of kitchen paper was attached to the wall, and tore off a few sheets.

'Here,' she said to Jonathan. 'Dry your eyes and blow your nose and tell me what's wrong.'

'Nothing,' said Jonathan, after a bit of snorting and wiping. 'I was hungry so I came to raid the cupboard. That's all.'

'That's why I came, too,' said Bianca. 'But I'm not crying. You don't cry because you're hungry. There must be something else the matter.'

Bianca started to eat a chocolate biscuit.

'I can't tell you.' Jonathan was still sniffy.

'Why not?'

'Because.'

'Because why?'

'Because you'd laugh.'

'Wouldn't.'

'Bet you would.'

'If Bianca says she won't laugh,' said Dodger, 'then she won't.'

Jonathan's mouth fell open. 'Was that your teddy bear talking?'

'Yes, yes,' said Bianca, taking a second biscuit,

'but that doesn't matter now. Just tell me what's wrong.'

'Why do you want to know?' Jonathan eyed her with suspicion.

Bianca sighed. Why were boys all so stupid?

'Because,' she explained, 'if you tell me what's wrong, I may be able to help you.'

'Doubt it.' Tears came into Jonathan's eyes again.

'Well, I might,' said Bianca. 'It's worth a try, isn't it?'

'OK,' said Jonathan. 'You asked for it. I'm homesick. That's all. You can't help me, and what's more, I bet you tell everyone.'

'I won't tell anyone,' said Bianca. 'I said I wouldn't. Don't you ever listen? And I can help. Did you bring a teddy bear or similar? Like it said we had to on the list?'

'You must be joking. That's baby stuff. I haven't played with my teddy bear for years and years.'

'You have got one, then?'

'Oh, yes. He's white and squashy. He's called Squelch.' Jonathan blushed and whispered, 'I wish I *had* brought him now.'

Bianca said, 'Well, you can borrow Dodger if you like.'

Dodger coughed loudly. 'I'm not consulted, I see. Just passed around from pillar to post as if I had no opinions of my own.'

'Oh, I'm sorry, Dodger, honestly. I *meant* to

ask you, I did really. You don't mind being Jonathan's bear just for a bit, do you? He's in real need of a bear. You'd be doing something tremendously noble. Truly.'

'Oh, very well,' said Dodger, 'if it'll make everyone happy.'

'It will,' said Bianca. 'Thank you! Right.' She pulled out a chair and sat down next to Jonathan. 'Pass those biscuits over here.'

When the whole packet of biscuits had disappeared, Bianca and Jonathan looked around for something else to eat.

'What about cornflakes?' asked Bianca.

'I can't bear them without milk. Let's see if there's any milk in the fridge.' Jonathan suddenly stood very still, listening.

'Did you hear that?'

'What?'

'A sort of whispering, slithery noise. Listen!'

Bianca listened and nodded. She turned pale. This was surely a ghost. It sounded so slow and shuffling. It must be some ancient Thing, come up from the dank cellar dragging sheets of slime and old leaves behind it . . .

'Now what on earth,' said a quavering voice, 'is going on here at this hour of the night?'

Bianca felt all the breath she'd been holding rush out of her lungs at once.

'Oh, Mrs Page! I'm so glad to see you. And Mr Page. We thought you were ghosts.'

'We thought you were burglars,' said Mr Page. 'We don't hold with ghosts, not in this house. Well.' He sat down and turned to Mrs Page. 'That was a bit of a shock, dear, eh? Still, it's only children, so it's teachers' business, really. I wonder if we should report them? I daresay they'll be too tired after the night's shenanigans to go exploring waterfalls and such . . .'

'Oh, please,' said Bianca. 'Please don't tell them. We'll go to bed straight away. We were hungry, that's all. We didn't like what we had for supper, so we came to get biscuits . . . ' Her voice faded away.

'What did I tell you?' said Mrs Page, whose grey hair hung in a plait down her back, reminding Bianca of Filomena. 'If I've told Mr Page once, I've told him a hundred times. You get what you pay for. Those burgers your teachers brought with them are the cheapest you can get and they taste like it. You'd all have been better off with a couple of crusty loaves of bread and a chunk of Wensleydale.'

Bianca nodded. 'I'm very sorry we woke you up. We'll go back to our rooms now.'

'You'll do no such thing,' said Mrs Page. 'You'll sit in those chairs till I've made you a nice hot drink.'

A few minutes later, Bianca and Jonathan were drinking the best hot chocolate in the world. Mr Page had found a packet of marshmallows to float on top, and some chocolate sprinkles as well. Dodger was sitting quietly on Jonathan's lap.

'This is nice, dear,' said Mr Page. 'We should have this more often.'

Mrs Page explained to Bianca and Jonathan. 'I used to make hot chocolate for my own children, only they've grown up and gone down south now.'

'Do you miss them?' Jonathan asked. 'I miss my home and I've only been away about twelve hours.'

'Oh, you'll be right as rain tomorrow, lad,' said Mr Page. 'Once they've got you clambering over rocks. It's only in the dark, like, when you have time to stop and think ... that's when you go missing folk.' He nodded at Mrs Page. Me and the wife, we're all right in the summer, when the schools come, but the winters are long. I will say that. Long and lonely. Still,' he smiled, 'we've got each other. Mustn't grumble.'

'Right,' said Mrs Page. 'It's time you children were asleep. Off you go now and we'll do the dishes.'

'Thank you,' said Bianca. 'That was a really ace drink.'

'Yes, thank you,' said Jonathan. 'And you won't tell our teachers, will you?'

'No, lad, of course we won't. You take that teddy and get off to bed. That's a smashing

86

teddy, that is. Traditional. I don't hold with all these fancy new bears in peculiar colours myself. I like a proper teddy. That's what my children always had.'

'And quite right too!' said Dodger, under his breath. He'd been sitting quite still so as not to alarm the Pages. 'My sentiments exactly.'

Bianca went back to the girls' room and climbed quietly into her bunk. She could hear everyone breathing in their sleep. I wish, she thought, that I still had Dodger to talk to. How sad it must be for the Pages in the winter, with all those empty rooms and long, black corridors. What they needed was a pet, or something. Bianca sat up in bed and looked over at the windowsill, and grinned. It was a brilliant idea. She would swear everyone to secrecy – Jenny, Sarah, Tanya – all of them. The Pages would have a wonderful surprise.

'Cats,' she said softly into the darkness, 'sleep well. You'll need lots of energy in the morning. I'm planning a surprise.'

Next morning after breakfast, Bianca and her friends were quick to offer help to Mrs Page, who was supervising the washing-up. Mrs Dawes could be heard asking if anyone knew who had been at the chocolate biscuits.

'Can you hear miaowing?' asked Sarah. 'It sounds as though there's a cat outside the back door.'

'Probably the black tom from the next farm,' said Mrs Page. 'Open up, then, and let's give him a saucer of milk.'

Sarah opened the door, and two white cats with small roundish ginger spots all over them came in and wound themselves affectionately in and out of Mrs Page's legs as she stood at the sink.

'Oh, my goodness,' she said smiling. 'Aren't they pretty? They're not cats I've ever seen before. Listen to them purring. I think I'd better see what I've got that they can eat. Oh, they're lovely!'

'What's all this, then?' said Mr Page, coming into the kitchen. 'What's those cats doing there? Whose are they?'

'I've never seen hair or hide of them before,' said Mrs Page. 'And look, one's got a bit missing out of his ear.'

'And that other one's toe isn't too grand,' said Mr Page. 'Looks as if they've been in the wars. Well, we'd best put a notice in the *Reporter* and see if anyone claims them.'

Mrs Page looked crestfallen. 'But we can keep them till someone claims them, can't we?'

'Oh, aye,' said Mr Page. 'We can do that all right.'

He stared at the cats, who had found a warm place near the big boiler in the corner, and settled down there as if they had spent their whole lives at Henston Hall. 'It's a funny thing,' he said at last. 'I could swear I'd seen those two cats somewhere, but I'm blowed if I can remember where . . .'

He left the room, scratching his chin thoughtfully.

'We're going out now,' Bianca said to Mrs Page. 'To visit the waterfall. Don't worry about the cats. I'm quite sure no one will claim them.'

'You must know something I don't then,' said Mrs Page. 'I'm going to keep my fingers crossed, though. They're that pretty.'

Bianca giggled and waved as she left the room.

By the time the children left for home, the two cats had become the most important and cherished inhabitants of Henston Hall. During the day, they patrolled the frontiers of their territory, prowling round the garden, sniffing strange footprints in the grass. Whenever the children returned from an outing, the cats would be there to greet them. They were particularly fond of Bianca, and found their way into every photograph of her. They followed Mrs Page wherever she went.

'They curl up on either side of the fireplace in the evenings,' she told Bianca, 'for all the world like those china cats you see in antique shops.' Bianca smiled. Mrs Page continued, 'I'll have my work cut out looking after them. They're fussier than any of you children.'

As the coach made its way slowly down the hill towards the main road, Bianca looked back at Mrs Page, flanked by the cats.

'I wonder when they'll realize,' Sarah said, 'that those cats are just like the chipped ornaments they wrapped up and put away in the cupboard.'

'I don't think they ever will,' said Bianca. 'They must have put those china cats away so long ago, they've forgotten all about them ... or maybe the cats belonged to the people who were here before the Pages came.'

Just then, Mrs Dawes called out, 'Jonathan! What are you doing walking all over the coach? Didn't I tell all of you to stay in your seats? I thought I'd made myself quite clear.'

'Yes, Miss, I know, Miss, only there's something I've forgotten to give back to Bianca. I'll only be one second.'

Mrs Dawes sighed. 'Very well then, Jonathan. Just give it to her and go back and sit down, please.'

Jonathan dropped Dodger into Bianca's lap.

'Thanks for this,' he said. 'See you!'

'Hello, Dodger,' Bianca whispered. 'How are you?'

Dodger was spluttering. 'It's been the most frightful three days! That boy has simply no conversation whatsoever – and did you hear him call me "this?" "Thanks for this" – that's what he said. Some people just haven't the faintest notion of courtesy.'

'Well, you're back with me now,' said Bianca, 'and we'll soon be home.'

'Thank goodness for that,' said Dodger. 'They don't call it 'Home Sweet Home' for nothing, I now realize.'

He smiled at Bianca and turned to watch the landscape flying past the windows of the coach.

We Fantoras have had our share of Fame. The limelight has been turned on 58, Azalea Avenue more than once in the last few months, and I think it fair to say that on one occasion at least, I have been in the centre of the stage, so to speak. Last Christmas, Eddie attracted the attention of several newspapers and also of the local radio station with his Fruit Salad Tree, which was the talk of the Barton Bridge Estate. For a few weeks, we became quite used to having the house invaded by young people trailing wires and waving microphones and pulling notebooks out of handbags. Everyone had to answer questions, except for me, of course. The Press was not aware of my many talents. We were photographed, gathered round the Fruit Salad Tree, all grinning stupidly at the camera.

My own Fame, not to mention Fortune, is not something I have hurried to write about, but I feel that now is a good time, perhaps, to unfold the mystery that has surrounded the rather splendid studio portrait of me which hangs on the Family Wall.

Some months ago, Bianca and Marco finally revealed why it was that they'd been following me about.

'There's a competition, Ozzy,' Marco said. 'They need a cat to advertise something called "Purrfection – the food for cats who are purrfect." We have to send in a picture of you.'

'I will win it,' I said, 'because, of course, I am perfection as far as cats are concerned.'

'No, silly,' said Bianca. 'Not perfection. *Purr*fection. I think it's a kind of biscuit. There's also a normal kind of catfood called "Purrnickety . . . for cats who are purrfectionists".'

'Aren't I rather too old for this kind of *purr*formance?' I asked.

Bianca and Marco were too excited even to laugh at my rather witty joke.

'Nonsense,' said Bianca. 'You're very handsome, and we're going to take a lovely photo of you on Francesca's bed. Bet you you'll win.'

The photograph which the children sent to the competition *did* make me look rather endearing. I was curled up on Francesca's flower-printed duvet, and looking up at the camera. The whole effect was very artistic, I thought, and the judges must have agreed with me, because one day a stiff white envelope flew through the letter box and landed on the hall carpet. I was to be a Purrfection Cat. I was to be driven to a television studio to take part in the making of a short film which would advertise one of the Purrfection Range of products.

Such excitement! Such comings and goings and toings and froings! Bianca and Marco were allowed the day off school to accompany me to the television studio. Francesca did not wish to be left out, so she had the day off as well. Filomena came too, to keep an eye on all of us, and because, as she put it, 'I saw it days and days ago. I've been finding sparkly gold yarn in my hands over and over again recently and it's been knitting itself into star shapes all over the fabric. That must be you, Ozzy, the twinkling Star of the Family.'

I do not deny that I enjoyed the fuss that everyone made of me. To be universally admired is deeply gratifying, naturally, and I did like the enthusiastic sounds that all the television people made when they met me for the first time. Someone from the Purrfection Food Company was there too, a round, rather shiny person, tightly squeezed into a pale grey suit. I was stroked and petted and made much of, but for all that, it was an experience I will be happy not to repeat. I had never realized how much waiting around and doing nothing are involved when a film is being made. Cables are wriggling all over the floor, people are arranging the cushion you are to sit on, the lighting, the sound-levels – oh, the technical bits and pieces that go on are endless. Then at last it is time for a 'take' as it is called, and out you come under the bright lights and do your piece, little realizing that you will probably have to do it another fifty times before everyone is happy.

I stepped on to my purple cushion, and gave my best profile to the camera, as a disembodied voice filled the air with this message: 'Isn't he a Purrfect Poppet? That's why only Purrfection, the Purrfect Cat's favourite confection is good enough for him.' This was going to be my contribution to the promotion. A small tabby and white kitten had been cast as the 'Purrnickety Cat' and was waiting her turn under the gaze of the camera.

It took a whole day to make a film that only lasted thirty seconds, but I have to say that I like the way I looked on the television screen. I am naturally photogenic, it seems.

'We will send you some stills from the film,'

the director said as we left. 'And a cheque, of course. And a whole year's supply of the Purrfection Range of products. Thank you so much.'

'You were lovely, Ozzy,' Francesca said in the car on the way home. Rosie had come to fetch us from the studio. 'He was lovely, Mum. Everyone said so.'

'They called him a natural,' said Bianca.

'I've written a poem about him,' said Marco. 'Listen.

> *Ozzy is Purrfection.*
> *There's no arguing with that.*
> *Even Purrfect strangers say:*
> *'He's the Purrfect Cat. Hooray!'*

'Very good, dear,' said Rosie. 'You can tell me all about it when we get home.'

I enjoyed my moment of Fame and Fortune. I shall long remember the first time my film was shown on the television. The Collins's came in from next door for a small celebration, and Rosie cooked me my favourite salmon trout. Everyone said 'ooh' and 'aah' and 'how wonderful' and if the truth be told, I *was* rather magnificent, but one gets used to everything in the end, and now we don't even make a special effort to watch the advertisement every time it's on. Sometimes we catch a glimpse of it in the middle of another programme, but that is all. Nevertheless, the director was as good as his word, and sent us several still photographs, one of which has been framed and hangs on the wall to remind everyone of my moment of glory. As for the Purrfection Range of products, I regret to say I found them quite tasteless, but they were eaten in the end. Bianca and Marco take them round to the Garner family across the road in number 25 every time they are delivered. Their cat, Mason, will eat anything. He is a cat with whom I have struck up quite a friendship, and I was pleased to think that he will enjoy them for a whole year, thanks to me.

Mason Garner is not only a friend. He has also helped me in my task as a Narrator. There are a great many cats on the Barton Bridge Estate who are so busy rushing from garden to garden in a ceaseless pursuit of creatures smaller than themselves that one hardly even learns their names. Mason, on the other hand, spends hours and hours basking on the wall in front of his house, and he is a cat with whom one can have a civilized conversation. He is nearly as old as I am, and has a fund of memories on which to draw. Mr Garner used to be groundsman at the local Cricket Club before he retired, and Mason was the Cricket Club Cat, made much of by every visiting team, and petted by the Ladies Who Made The Teas. Naturally, he knows all about the game of cricket: all those tiny details which, I have to admit, I find so confusing. Oh, I thrill to the idea of wide, tree-bordered green pitches, elegant figures in white hitting that hard, red ball to the boundary, spectators clapping and eating dainty little sandwiches under a pale blue sky filled with cotton-wool clouds. I can read the score on a scoreboard, and I'm usually aware of a brilliant catch or a hundred runs or a stump being knocked out of the ground, but I am ignorant, I confess, of the finer points of the game. I don't know the difference between 'gully' and 'point', I couldn't tell you the significance of 'leg-breaks', 'off-breaks' and 'googlies', and 'Yorkers' and 'Chinamen' have me quite bewildered. I don't know the meaning of 'slow left arm' or 'round the wicket', and 'silly mid-on' and 'silly mid-off' simply make me laugh. But catching sight of Marco's team photograph on the Family Wall reminded me of a cricket match we had all been to watch, and the story of that match is one worth telling. I have made my way through the catflap and round to the front of the house to consult with Mason about cricketing details, and he has been most helpful. I'm ashamed to say that I had to hear the story from Marco himself, because while I was supposed to be watching the game, I was actually fast asleep. The thwack of leather on willow (Mason assures me that this is what cricket buffs say when they mean 'the ball hitting the bat') is very soothing. I therefore missed most of the action, opening my eyes only to partake of some light refreshment at the lunch interval.

Marco's team photograph! How pleased with themselves they all look! Marco seems particularly happy. He had never in his wildest dreams expected to be in the team, and it was only because two boys were absent through illness that he was chosen. He is standing at the end of the back row, on the left-hand side. Granville (star player of the team: opening batsman and Captain to boot) is sitting in the middle of the front row. He has yellow hair that glows. His sweater and teeth are sparkling white. He looks like an advertisement. But team photographs do not reveal the dramas of the afternoon. There were dark deeds afoot. There was to be a battle of Good versus Evil (in a small sort of way) but no one looking at this photograph would guess.

This has been what is known in cricketing circles as a 'run-up', so now let me bowl a title at you, closely followed by an opening paragraph.

The Invisible (Twelfth) Man

Marco came bounding home from school one day in May with the most exciting news.

'I've got,' he cried, 'the most tremendously exciting news.'

'I know,' said Rosie. 'Filomena told us already.'

'Filomena? What did she say? How did she know?'

'Silly!' Auntie Varvara said. 'How does she

always know? From the knitting of course. She says you're going to be in a cricket match. Is it true?'

Marco sat down and stuck his tongue out at no one in particular.

'It's not fair. I wanted to tell you. What kind of knitting was it? I never heard of cricketing knitting.'

'Cables in white,' said Filomena, who had just come downstairs ready for her afternoon session on the trampoline. 'You only ever get this kind of cable on a cricket sweater or pullover. And there was a border as well, in the school colours. Have you been picked for the First Eleven? Are you going to be playing for the school? You clever boy!'

'I'm the Twelfth Man,' said Marco, 'which is ace. I get to be one of the team, and if no one is hurt, I won't even have to play. Jackson and Young are ill, so they chose me.'

'Why don't you want to play?' asked Eddie. It was a Wednesday afternoon, and the shop was shut. Eddie had come home to do some serious pottering in the greenhouse. 'I thought you loved cricket.'

'Well, I do,' said Marco, 'to watch and read about, but I'm a bit scared of that ball. It's ever so hard and it always looks as if it's coming right at you. So this is the best thing possible. I can just be there, in the pavilion and everything. And

I get to take drinks out to the middle if anyone wants them. Will you all come and watch? It's on Saturday, and it's against St Peter's and if we win we've got a place in the finals of the Schools Cup, and we *will* win, I know. We've got the Great Granville.'

'Who's he?' Rosie asked.

This turned out to be a mistake, because Marco started to tell us all about him at great length: his batting average, his uncanny prowess at hitting sixes, his many brilliant innings for the school. We all listened politely at first, but gradually our eyes glazed over and Francesca was seen to yawn loudly. Marco took the hint and brought his monologue to an end with a sentence which summed up all the rest, 'He's a bit like David Gower.'

It seemed that Granville could win the game all by himself. Scouts from the County Youth Team were coming to the match, so why, said Marco, didn't we make a Family Outing of it?

A Family Outing, in this family, is exactly that. No one is allowed to stay away. Monkey and Leopard come in a special box, Rosie is put in charge of the picnic, and even cats who would rather be snoozing peacefully on a sunny cushion are not spared. My cat basket is brought out of the garage, and I am put into it. It is a very luxurious basket, with widely-spaced bars to look through and plenty of soft padding to rest on.

102

Nevertheless one is not free to roam when one is shut into it.

'You can come out at the Club,' said Francesca, 'and sit on my lap if you like. I have to go to make sure the weather doesn't spoil things.'

I nodded. If there is one thing about cricket which I have learned over the years, it is this: wherever a match is being played, there is a very strong chance of rain. Francesca quite rightly saw herself as the most important person on either side. Mason has more than once suggested that she offer her services to the groundsman at Old Trafford.

Auntie Varvara was persuaded to lay aside her wedding magazines and swatches of fabric and come and support the Otter Street team. She put on a sunhat for the occasion and packed in her handbag (nestling against the latest crop of love-letters) a novel entitled *Deirdre's Desperate Desires* in case the game was less than engrossing. Rosie made a traditional sort of lunch: bloater paste sandwiches and slabs of fruit cake and apples for everyone. Auntie Varvara had a couple of barm cakes filled with assorted vegetation and there were flasks of hot drinks and bottles of fizzy cold ones. Filomena brought her knitting-bag but did not expect to be able to predict the score, even though Marco begged her to do her best.

'I can only,' said Filomena, 'predict general

103

sorts of things, not exact numbers of runs and wickets.'

I was amazed. Fancy Filomena knowing about runs and wickets!

'I can tell you one thing though,' she said to Marco on the morning of the match. 'There's going to be some dirty work. I'm doing twisted stitches . . . that always means deception of some kind, so keep your ears and eyes open.'

The game began at half past ten. Otter Street lost the toss and St Peter's chose to bat first. All the Otter Street boys dispersed to their positions on the field, except, of course, for Marco. He waited in the pavilion with the team from St Peter's, ready to watch the game.

We spectators were busy spectating. That is to say: Rosie was thinking about whether her students could possibly manage next week's Magic Recipe, Francesca (who had not been called upon to stop any rain) was chatting to Monkey and Leopard, and Bianca was eyeing one of the trees, wondering how far up it she could climb. Auntie Varvara had dipped into her novel and from the way her mouth was hanging open, I could tell that Deirdre's Desires were going to be very Desperate indeed. Eddie, I could see, was miles away, probably considering the knotty problem of Auntie Varvara's wedding bouquet. She *did* want such a complicated mixture of flowers. Filomena's needles were slowing down . . . soon her eyes would be closed, which seemed like a good idea to me, so I closed mine as well.

Marco, however, was wide-awake. He was more wide-awake than he had ever been in his life. Filomena had been right, and there was something afoot. He'd been sitting quietly, unnoticed, in a corner, minding his own business. The Captain of the St Peter's team and two of his cronies were muttering. Marco could hear what they were saying.

'It's that Granville,' said Crony One. 'He can win all by himself. We're going to have to see to him.'

'We haven't got the bowling power, that's the trouble,' said Crony Two. At that moment, the Captain caught sight of Marco.

'Shut up!' he said. 'Come in the changing room. There's Otter Street ears flapping round here!'

They swaggered off. Marco sat trembling in his chair. What should he do? He had to find out what those three were up to. This must be the cheating Filomena had mentioned. He knew how he could do it. He could use his own special gift and become invisible. Marco found it very easy to disappear. He simply made himself feel transparent, and then, almost immediately, he began to disappear, just like a drawing being rubbed out. But what if one of the Otter Street team got hit on the head while Marco was being invisible? No one would be able to find the Twelfth Man, and then where would he be? He hesitated for only a second. It was a risk he would have to take. He made himself vanish into thin air and folded his clothes neatly on the chair. Then he ran into the changing room and sat down beside the St Peter's boys.

'Right,' the Captain was saying. 'I've got a plan. I'm going to put Watson on to bowl when Granville comes in. As he'll be bowling slow, you,' he nodded at Crony One, 'keeping wicket, can stand up right near the stumps, and when you see Granville step back, to play defensively off the back foot, you can flick a bail off and appeal; we'll say Granville stepped on his wicket or touched the stumps with his bat, or something. Clever or what?' The Captain chortled.

'Dead clever,' said Crony Two. 'No one'll ever guess. And once Granville's out, the rest won't make twenty runs between them.'

Marco couldn't believe his ears. St Peter's were going to cheat. They had a plan. He didn't know how he was going to foil this plan, but foil it he would. He had the rest of the St Peter's innings to thing of something. It looked as though he would have to become invisible again, and it would be harder to do with his own schoolmates lolling around the pavilion. He'd have to find an excuse to leave the room. He'd worry about that later. Now he had to get into his clothes and be sitting down when the St Peter's gang came out of the changing-room.

St Peter's were all out for 114 runs. After the lunch interval, it was Otter Street's turn to bat. The Great Granville had put his pads on and was ready for action. So was Otter Street's other opening batsman, Andrews.

'Good luck,' said the rest of the team and off they went. Marco could hear the crowd clapping. There was a small balcony outside the pavilion, and everyone gathered there to watch their hero. Marco heaved a sigh of relief. Every eye was on Granville, and as usual, Granville was worth watching. He did everything right, playing each shot to perfection: he hooked and drove, executed one particularly fierce square-cut. On several pleasing occasions the ball made its way to the boundary.

Marco knew he had to hurry. He disappeared at once, and left his clothes to fall into a heap where he'd been standing. He then ran to the wicket and stood behind the wicket-keeper. When the St Peter's Captain put Watson on to bowl, Marco began to shake. What he had thought of doing seemed to him foolproof in the pavilion, but now it looked both uncomfortable and danger-ous. His idea was to stand to the side of the stumps, tucked between the wicket-keeper and Granville. As Granville was batting, he would hold the bails down with his bare (invisible) hands. He would have to do it for every ball that was bowled at Granville, because he did not know in advance when the chance would come for the wicket-keeper (or wicked-keeper, as Marco now thought of him) to put a crafty finger out and flick one of the bails off. He also had to be careful not to cheat himself. If the unthinkable were to happen, if a ball *did* manage to hit the wicket, then he must do nothing to interfere with it. He would have to remove his hands from the bails at once. Granville would then have been bowled fair and square.

Poor Marco! He never realized how tiring it was on the hands, keeping them in one position for a long time. He felt a little like the Dutch boy who put his finger in the dyke to hold back the floodwater. Ball after ball came trundling up the pitch, and Marco trembled. What if one went completely in the wrong direction and hit him? Things didn't hurt him when he was invisible quite so much as they did when he was all there, but still a cricket ball would be a little painful even in his present condition. There was no time to worry about such things. He had to keep his eyes open . . . and yes, this was it! It was happening. As Granville stepped back defensively, for perhaps the fourth or fifth time in his innings, the wicked-keeper's left hand, in its thick glove, darted out to dislodge a bail. The bail remained exactly where it was, with the weight of Marco's fingers on it. The wicked-keeper looked as though he couldn't believe his eyes. He shook his head in bewilderment. At the end of the over, the Captain approached him for a whispered chat. Marco crept up and listened.

'What happened?' said the Captain. 'That was a perfect chance and you made a mess of it. That's typical.'

'I tried!' squeaked the wicked-keeper. 'I *did* try. I couldn't flick the bail off. It was stuck.'

'Stuck?' The Captain's mouth dropped open. 'What with? Superglue? Pull the other one, it's got bells on it!'

'No, honestly,' said the wicked-keeper. 'It was. Not with Superglue, of course not. It felt more as if . . . ' His words faded away.

'As if what? We're starting.'

'As if someone was holding them down.'

'Right,' said the Captain. 'They've got the Invisible Man on their side, I suppose.'

Marco giggled. He couldn't help himself. The Captain said to the wicked-keeper, 'Was that you giggling?'

'No,' said the wicked-keeper. 'I thought it was you.'

'Not got a lot to giggle about, have I? Seeing as we've practically lost the game, thanks to you.'

He stalked off to the slips, muttering.

Twice more the wicked-keeper tried to cheat Granville out of his well-deserved triumph. Marco stopped him each time, and each time the keeper looked more baffled. At length, Granville was out legitimately – caught at gully for 58 runs – and Marco was relieved to be able to stand up straight and take his hands off the stumps. He followed his hero back to the pavilion and shared in the applause echoing round the ground.

When he got to the pavilion, everyone was looking for him.

'Fantora! Where *is* he when you need him? It's the last time I'm going to suggest him for the team,' muttered the Otter Street Captain.

Marco waited until everyone was watching the game again, and then got dressed as quickly as he could. He went up to one of the players.

'Were you looking for me?' he said smiling.

'Yes, you little wally, where ever have you been? We've been asked to help set out the tea, for the end of the match. You can do it.'

Otter Street beat St Peter's by 27 runs. The two teams came in to take tea, and Marco, going round with a plateful of chocolate fingers, made it his business to overhear a conversation between the St Peter's Captain and his wicket-keeper.

The Captain was moaning, 'I've got a keeper that's half asleep. That's what went wrong.'

'I *wasn't* asleep. Those bails were stuck. You don't know. You never tried to get them off. It's easy for you to talk.'

Marco grinned. He took his plate over to where Granville was standing, surrounded by a crowd of his admirers. He was saying, 'It was really weird but I felt there was someone standing behind me the whole time I was batting.'

'There was,' said one of the admirers. 'It was their wicket-keeper!'

Everyone laughed except Granville, who was looking dazed.

'Apart from the wicket-keeper, I mean,' he said. 'Someone else. I heard him . . . it . . . breathing a couple of times. I'm sure I did. Nothing will convince me there was nobody there.'

Everybody nodded. Granville was a hero. If he said there was somebody there, then maybe there was. Maybe it was a Force from Outer Space or something. That was Andrews' bright suggestion. In any case, Granville was more admired than ever. Now he was a hero with a touch of the supernatural about him. Marco felt very proud and only a little peeved that no one in the team would ever know what he'd done for Otter Street that day. His reward was the school's eventual triumph in the Inter-School Trophy. Mason assures me that winning is of secondary importance. He recited a little verse to me on one occasion, and although I cannot remember it exactly, its message was clear: what matters is not who wins or loses, but how you play the game. We in the Family all agreed that Marco had played most bravely, and that it was well worth having a stiff back from all that bending over, in order to see the Baddies brought low.

Soon, the Family will be back at 58, Azalea Avenue, and the house will once again ring with its usual music of voices, laughter and shouting. Doors will slam and cutlery will rattle, songs will be sung and arguments will break out when they are least expected. Life will return to normal. The only quiet place will once again be Eddie's greenhouse. I think of it as an oasis: a peaceful shady spot full of growing things where you are unlikely to hear anything more dramatic than the soft gurglings of water from the sink in the corner.

In the evenings and at weekends, Eddie spends a great deal of his time down at the greenhouse and I sometimes go with him. The things he does there are a mystery to me. I watch him transferring plants from one pot to another; I see him sprinkle them with substances I have never seen before and whose names I do not know; and I hear him talking to every new shoot that sprouts out of the magic potting compost he has devised.

From where I am presently sitting, about halfway up the stairs, I can see almost the only photograph on the whole Wall to show Eddie on his own. It was taken at this year's Barton Bridge Flower Festival and Eddie is flanked by two – no, I shall not say what he is flanked by. That must remain a surprise for the moment, but he looks happier than I have ever seen him look in a photograph. Usually, the appearance of a camera anywhere near him has him hiding behind someone, peeping from round the corner of somewhere. In other words, he is normally hardly visible at all. But here he is, in this picture, full-length and facing forward, and on either side stand his beloved ... well, I shall tell the story and all will be revealed.

In the few weeks before Auntie Varvara's wedding, Eddie's greenhouse activities intensified.

'I don't know how I'm going to manage everything, Ozzy, and that's a fact. Varvara keeps changing her mind. She says it's a woman's privilege, but I reckon three times a week is pushing it.'

I indicated my agreement, and Eddie went on. He is at his chattiest in the greenhouse, which is why I am the one who hears most of what he has to say. The rest of the Family hardly ever venture further than the end of the lawn.

'First, we have to redesign the garden for the wedding. One day, Varvara wants something out of the Arabian nights, the next day she fancies something Elizabethan, or else it's a medieval rose-garden, or a Japanese one. My head is reeling. I said to her last week, that's it, Varvara, I said. Tell me what you want now and DON'T CHANGE YOUR MIND AGAIN! These things take time, I told her, and I need every day between now and your wedding day if I'm to make a go of it. If you don't decide finally, what you'll end up with is what's out there now: a perfect example of Northern Suburban. That pulled her up short, Ozzy, I can tell you. So at least we know where we are and what we've got to do.'

I didn't have to ask what Auntie Varvara had decided on. Eddie told me straight away.

'She wants something Italian, she says. As a compliment to the Lupinos. Lots of vine trellises, and long tables covered with white cloths and Chianti bottles everywhere. She wonders if I've possibly got time for a gnarled olive tree. I told her that was going to be a bit difficult, and we compromised on a couple of small cypresses. They do give a place a very Mediterranean look,

I think. Still, at least I know where I am now, so I'm better off than I was before.'

No sooner had Eddie settled the matter of the garden with his sister, than the Bouquet Problem began to preoccupy him.

'She wants a bit of everything, Ozzy. Blood red roses, white gardenias, and (this is a bit of a poser, I have to admit), peacock blue lilies . . . a kind of deep turquoise, she calls it. I told her I'd never seen a lily that colour, and she just smiled and said, "Oh, you're so clever, Eddie, I'm sure you'll think of something."'

From the day that Auntie Varvara told him about her bouquet, Eddie worked long hours in the greenhouse every evening. The hardest item was the turquoise lilies. He started with white lilies and tried everything: ink, food colouring, cut-up lengths of knitting wool in a particularly vibrant shade of peacock blue. Nothing worked. Then, in a moment of inspiration, he added certain items to the soil surrounding a yellow lily, and on the very next day, all its petals had become turquoise: clear bluey-green streaked with a darker shade of the same colour.

'Magnificent!' said Eddie. 'I must run and fetch Varvara and the others.'

On this occasion, everyone trooped down from the house to see Auntie Varvara's special wedding lily.

'Oh, Eddie,' said the blushing bride-to-be when

she saw it. 'It's the most wonderful thing you've ever done. It's exactly what I wanted. Thank you!' She clasped Eddie in her arms. As she was wearing a floral dress with long, floaty sleeves, her poor brother was nearly suffocated in her embrace.

He struggled out of the material at last and said, 'I shall call this variety "Varvara" after you. I'm sure I shall be asked for it in the shop when people round here catch a glimpse of your bouquet.'

'But how,' asked Filomena, 'did you get that colour? It really is very striking.'

Eddie touched the side of his nose with his finger.

'Trade secrets,' he chuckled, and winked at me.

I knew what it was, because I was on the spot when Eddie thought of it. I knew that he would tell the others the formula in his own good time, so I do not feel I am doing anything dreadful by disclosing it now. The magic ingredient was a small bottle of Welsh mineral water, made of royal blue glass. Eddie smashed the bottle into small pieces, then ground the glass until it was a fine powder. This he mixed into the soil and the result was perfection.

With the problematic side of Auntie Varvara's bouquet out of the way, Eddie could concentrate on his Italian garden. He was thinking so hard about that that he didn't notice what he was doing as he went about his tidying up while the evening turned to night. I saw it, although I didn't realize what the result would be.

I saw him gathering flowers together, and putting them into vases. Roses, peonies and tulips in one bunch, gladioli, freesia and carnations in another, then one of marigolds, sweet williams and geraniums. Times and seasons, I knew, were of no concern to Eddie. He knew how to grow anything, anytime, anywhere. I can remember thinking: what pretty combinations, and then I forgot all about them. The flowers stood together on the shelf, and the days passed and no one looked at them. They faded. They withered. They died and no one took any notice. Eddie was hard at work on his vine. Then one day he happened to glance in the direction of the shelf which held up the vases of decayed stems and leaves and petals.

'Ozzy!' he whispered with awe in his voice. 'Come and look at this.'

Obediently, I padded over to peer at what Eddie was so excited about. I have to say I found it difficult to enthuse.

'Do you notice anything?' Eddie asked. 'Can you see these little green sprouting things on these dead stems over here? I'm not sure, but I think they may be the beginning of something special.'

He then removed the green shoots (which I confess I had difficulty in seeing very well) and planted them in three medium-sized pots.

117

Plants take time to grow. You have to watch them every day, water them and wait to admire the blooms. That's what we did, Eddie and I, but thanks to the magic of storytelling, I can save my readers from any further suspense. The little green shoots became Eddie's pride and joy: Bouquet Bushes. That is what he called them.

'It's a very simple notion, Ozzy,' he told me. 'I don't know why I never thought of it before. Each bush has three different kinds of flower growing on it, do you see? Brilliant! Wait till they see it at the Barton Bridge Flower Festival! They'll never get over this, mark my words. It's a Gold Medal for me this year, Ozzy. You can bet on it.'

And Eddie was right. The proof is hanging on the Family Wall for all to see: Eddie wearing a Gold Medal round his neck, and standing between two of his Bouquet Bushes, on each of which you can see quite clearly three different varieties of flower. Perhaps the most stunning Bouquet bush of all was the one Eddie went on to create for Auntie Varvara's wedding: red roses, white gardenias and the Varvara lily in all its turquoise glory.

I am not a Narrator who trembles and quakes very often, but I do so now at the thought of the task that lies before me. There is so much to tell that I intend to divide my account of The Wedding into two. I shall call the first part Preparations.

Preparations

For anyone who wishes to lead a quiet life, I have two words of advice: AVOID WEDDINGS! I have come to the conclusion that the process of getting married takes about a month and that it is not the ceremony itself that disrupts everything, but all the bits and pieces leading up to The Day. It's true, Auntie Varvara had been warning us. Ever since last Christmas she has muttered and murmured about 'so many things to attend to' but it wasn't until about three weeks before the wedding that the rest of us became involved as well. Before that, Auntie Varvara had been pleasurably occupied seeing to the printing of the invitations, going off every week for her fitting with Madame Liliane, chatting to Eddie about garden plans, and dreaming of her bouquet. The rest of us thought about the wedding from time to time, but it did not actually affect our daily lives. All that changed, and I was the first member of the Family to notice.

Presents

This was the first sign. Presents began arriving by every post. Interesting-looking boxes turned out to hold boring items such as toasters, coffee-pots, mugs or ornaments. The boxes were frequently flattened and taken to the recycling skip before I had had time to curl up in them for a short nap. Most of them were too small even to get into. Surfaces I used to enjoy sitting on from time to time were heaped with bed-linen, tea-towels and tablemats with pictures of castles on them. There were fewer and fewer places round the house where a sedate and elderly cat could rest for a moment. It was most unsettling.

'What can we get Auntie Varvara?' Bianca asked her mother one day. 'She's been given everything already.'

'And anyway,' said Marco, 'we haven't got huge amounts of money.'

'You can club together,' said Rosie. 'All three of you. And Auntie Varvara will love whatever you give her. You know she will. She loves almost everything.'

That was true. I had seen her exclaim ecstatically over a set of cut-glass fruit dishes, and sigh extravagantly after just one glimpse of a rather ordinary alarm clock.

'I've bought my present,' said Francesca. 'I saw it in a shop and I asked Filomena for the money.'

'What is it?'

'It's lots and lots of bath pearls, like little pink hearts, packed in a heart-shaped box. Auntie Varvara loves anything that has pink hearts on it.'

That was also true.

'Fancy thinking of something all by yourself,' Bianca said. She sounded even more glum than she had before. 'You might have told us.'

I tried to cheer her up by telling her that I would help her and Marco to think of something.

'Thank you,' she said. 'And you can join in the present, Ozzy. It'll be from the three of us.'

We did find something in the end. It may not have been Auntie Varvara's most expensive present, but I would most certainly have preferred it to any number of household appliances. We found a most beautiful notebook, with covers marbled in shades of blue and mauve and brown, in which the bride could write her innermost thoughts. To the notebook we added a shiny black pen with a silver nib. Auntie Varvara will now be able to record every moment of her new life for Posterity.

Filomena's present had been ready for a long time. She had made the young couple a bedspread: lacy patterns worked in cream cotton yarn. I spotted fans and trellises, and cables and chevrons and ladders, panels of twisted vines, crossed cables, feather stitch . . . oh, wherever you looked there was something strange and exquisite to wonder at.

'I've surpassed myself, Ozzy,' said Filomena. 'There's everything you could possibly think of in this bedspread. It's exactly like life. Ups and downs, changes, disappointments, calm and quiet days, and days when you don't know whether you're coming or going. I've put them all into this.'

I wondered aloud why there were none of Filomena's usual bright singing colours in the bedspread, and she thought a long time before answering. Finally she said, 'The colours of her life when she leaves this house, Ozzy, will be up to her. Up to her and Remo. I can tell you many things that are going to happen, but not even I can predict what Varvara's life will be like when she's married. That will be for them both to decide. But I'll tell you a secret, Ozzy.' She leaned forward and whispered in my ear. 'The colours will arrive in the bedspread one by one, first in one little spot and then in another. After a year or two of marriage, it'll be as colourful as a patchwork. Don't breathe a word, Ozzy. Let it be a surprise for Varvara when she's far away from her poor old mum. She'll be tickled pink to see her bedspread transforming itself before her very eyes.' Filomena chuckled and I promised to say nothing.

The cake

As well as the presents, there was the cake to worry about. Rosie was in charge of that, of course, but what it might look like was the subject of much heated debate.

'Traditional,' said Auntie Varvara.

'Like a fairytale castle,' said Francesca.

'What about Dracula's Castle?' asked Rosie. 'To remind you of Transylvania, where you and Remo met.'

'I don't want grey icing on my wedding cake,' Auntie Varvara sniffed. 'Can't you just make an ordinary four-tier wedding cake? Look, there's one in this magazine.' She scrabbled about in the latest issue of *Best for Brides* and we all looked carefully at the photograph. The tiny statues of

123

the bride and groom on the very highest tier seemed to be wearing very fixed grins, but the cake did look extremely pretty.

'If that's what you would like,' said Rosie, 'then that is what you shall have.'

She set to work, and by the day of the wedding, the cake was standing in pride of place in the dining-room. It *did* look exactly like Auntie Varvara's magazine cake, except that the little plastic figures of the bride and groom (which in the photograph were standing under a canopy of roses) were, in Rosie's version, just about to go into a miniature Gothic castle spun from the finest white sugar that twinkled and sparkled where the light caught it, as though it were fashioned from ice and fire.

'How will everyone fit in?' Marco asked, as the invitations were answered and everyone agreed to come. 'How can you squash fifty people into a little house like this?'

'Silly!' said Bianca. 'We're having the party outside. Francesca will make the day as sunny as it would be in Italy, and everyone will go into the garden. They'll walk about on the lawn and the tables with the food on them will be all round the edges. It'll be great.'

'When are the Lupinos coming?' Francesca wanted to know, 'and how will we speak to them if they're Italian, and where are they going to sleep?'

'They're booked into the Meadowbank Hotel,'

said Marco. 'Auntie Varvara told me. The Belmont wasn't posh enough for them. They're used to nothing but the best.'

'Gosh!' said Francesca. 'But how will we talk to them?'

'They all speak English, that's how,' said Bianca. 'Because of spending years and years in America.'

'They must be jolly rich,' said Francesca, 'to fly to a wedding in an aeroplane and only stay two days and then go back.'

'They *are* jolly rich,' said Bianca, 'but they'd have come anyway. Remo is the Contessa's favourite child. That's what Auntie Varvara told me.'

Outfits

Both the girls and Marco had been taken by Auntie Varvara to Madame Liliane's flat to have their outfits attended to.

'I know it's a Registry Office wedding,' said Auntie Varvara, 'but that's no reason for me to do without attendants. Bianca and Francesca in turquoise and Marco in black and white – they'll look wonderful and bring out the white and turquoise in my bouquet as well.'

Madame Liliane had been delighted to meet the children, and turned only a little pale when Bianca, in a rather dull moment, brought to life a small collection of wooden animals which stood on a shelf above the sewing-machine table. She managed to keep smiling as she watched three camels, two donkeys, an antelope, a giraffe and a family of elephants frolicking among her materials, jumping from one bookshelf to another, and hiding behind her curtains. Nothing the Fantoras did could surprise her any more.

'Goodness,' she chuckled rather half-heartedly as one of the camels appeared under the hem of Francesca's skirt which she was pinning to the right length. 'Whatever next?'

'Bianca, honestly,' sighed Auntie Varvara. 'This place is much too small for these tricks. Put the animals back on the shelf at once!'

Bianca did as she was told, thinking how boring the fitting was going to be with nothing to cheer it up. Madame Liliane secretly heaved a sigh of relief. She failed to understand, however, why no one batted an eyelid when Marco couldn't be found.

'Don't worry, Liliane,' said Auntie Varvara. 'He's just disappeared for a while. He'll be back.'

'Does he,' Madame Liliane enquired, 'disappear often?'

'It's when he doesn't like what's happening,' said Bianca. 'And he doesn't like having clothes fitted.'

'Marco!' Auntie Varvara said (into the empty

air, as far as Madame Liliane could see), 'come back this minute and let's get the sleeves of this shirt right. This is my wedding and I want you to look nice.'

'Here I am,' said Marco, 'so stop fussing. I've been here all the time.'

And there he was, sitting in the armchair in the corner. Madame Liliane shook her head and rubbed her eyes. What was wrong with her? Was she working too hard? She could have sworn that only two seconds ago that armchair had been empty. She took a deep breath.

'All the children,' she said, 'will look wonderful.'

The Photographer

'The photographs,' Auntie Varvara announced a few weeks before the wedding, 'will be taken by my friend Arnold.'

'What friend Arnold?' asked Filomena. 'I've never heard you speak of him. Who is he and why is he called Arnold?'

'People have to be called something,' said Auntie Varvara, 'and we shouldn't make fun of his name. It's Peaswallop. Arnold Peaswallop.'

Bianca, Marco and Francesca burst out laughing and the entire table was covered with a fine spray of milk and shredded pieces of cornflake.

'Children! Stop it at once!' said Rosie sternly.

'This wedding is making you all soft in the head.'
Then she giggled. 'Oh, I'm sorry, but I can't help
it. Peaswallop! Poor chap. You'd think he'd
change it, wouldn't you?'

'He's a very good photographer. He has a
small studio on Watford Road.'

'If you say so, Varvara dear,' said Filomena.
'We'll have to trust you.'

'But I should warn you,' Auntie Varvara said,
'that he is rather quiet and not very cheerful.'

'As long as he takes good pictures,' said Eddie
from behind the pages of *The Barton Bugle*, 'that's
all we care about. We will not expect him to be a
comedian.'

As a Narrator it is my duty to tell you that
Auntie Varvara was understating the case. Arnold
Peaswallop looked as though he had recently
struggled out of a coffin. He had straggly black
hair, a complexion somewhere between ashen and
pallid with tinges of green here and there, and he
wore clothes of no fixed shape or colour, but
which might once have been an oversized suit in
clerical grey worn over assorted waistcoats and
cardigans. He looked at us all out of sunken,
mud-brown eyes behind rimless glasses and did a
lot of breathing through his mouth. He did *not*
inspire confidence.

'He looks like a zombie,' Francesca said with
the honesty of the very young.

'If he is one of the Undead,' said Filomena,

'I'm not having him in the house and that's that.'
She stood up very straight. 'I draw the line at the
Undead.'

'Don't be ridiculous, Mother,' said Auntie Varvara. 'He's not one of the Undead. He's from
Derbyshire. He just spends a lot of time in his
darkroom, so he's a little pale, that's all. He's
really a very talented photographer. You'll see.'

A few days after we had met Arnold Peaswallop, I noticed that Eddie had bought several rolls
of film for his camera.

'Better to be safe than sorry, Ozzy,' he said,
and winked.

The Lupinos

All my skills as a Narrator will not, I fear, be
enough to describe the effect that the arrival of
the Lupinos had on our household. Imagine a
field of ordinary grass that suddenly finds four
exotic orchids growing in it. Or think of a pet
show, with everyone quietly walking round with
their cat or dog or rabbit, when all at once there's
a tiger in the parade, and an elephant and a zebra
and a crocodile. If you saw such a thing, your
jaw would drop, and you would not believe your
eyes. Just so did we feel when we first saw the
Lupinos.

Auntie Varvara went to the airport to meet
them, and they all turned up at Azalea Avenue in

a car that Remo had hired: a shocking-pink lim-
ousine, 'even bigger than Frilly Dilys's Dad's',
as Francesca so precisely put it. The Collins's,
the Garners, oh, half the neighbours at least
came out of their houses to stare at it, and were
rewarded by the sight of the Lupino family step-
ping out of it. They were all clearly quite used
to being stared at by crowds of admirers, and
waved in a regal fashion to the assembled multitudes (only about twelve people, in fact, but
that counts as multitudes in Azalea Avenue) as
they strolled up the garden path and into
number 58.

I cannot begin to convey the kissing and squealing and yelping and sighing and exclaiming that
went on. The boot of the pink car opened to
reveal suitcase after suitcase. I counted eight, and
was greatly relieved that they would not be taking
up space in our house. Still, the one carrying the
presents had to be located of course, and it was
right at the bottom, so all the others needed to be
taken out and put back, and while all this was
happening, the noise and laughter and general
hilarity did not cease for a second. The children
had never been kissed so much in their lives.

'Italians are very friendly,' Auntie Varvara
hissed at Marco, when she saw he was beginning
to disappear around the edges. 'And they adore
children. Besides,' she went on, 'they're going to
be part of our Family.'

Marco restored himself and prepared for further embraces.

And what of the Lupinos themselves, when the presents had been found, and the front door shut and everyone was sitting in the lounge having a reviving cup of tea? Well, Remo was just as I expected: very hairy, with large white teeth. He was dressed in a cream linen suit. He seemed very fond of Auntie Varvara, narrowing his eyes and puckering his mouth up into a kissing position every time his gaze fell on her, which was often. He seemed to be a cheery sort of fellow, laughing heartily at everything. Zenobia, his sister, behind her dark glasses, looked as though she had stepped out of one of Auntie Varvara's magazines. She had a glossy red mouth, long red fingernails, and was wearing rings and brooches that caught the light and dazzled you with their brilliance.

'*She's* glamorous,' Bianca whispered to Francesca.

'I can see that, silly,' said Francesca. 'I don't need to be told.'

The Contessa, Remo and Zenobia's mother, was as glamorous as her daughter, only older. Where Zenobia wore scarlet and black, the Contessa was draped in beige and dusty pink; where Zenobia's jewels flashed, the Contessa's gems glowed discreetly.

'We are so happy to be here with you,' she

131

said, smiling graciously. 'We are so loving the English tea!'

The Contessa's brother, known only as Zio Giovanni, had taken a fancy to Filomena. He was a tall, whiskery man with amber-coloured eyes under bushy white eyebrows, and he turned all his charm on Filomena till, as she said later, 'I didn't know what was happening. No one has taken so much interest in me for years and years.'

The visitors brought wonderful presents: silk scarves, bottles of oil pressed from olives grown on the Lupino estates, special biscuits and beautifully dressed dolls for the girls. I was touched that they had remembered me, with a few tins of the most delicious seafood titbits. By the time they left for their hotel, we were all exhausted.

'Aren't they nice?' Eddie said. 'I really liked them. They seem . . . well . . . quite normal in spite of being so rich.'

Auntie Varvara laughed. 'They *are* nice,' she said, 'but they have their little ways, believe me. For example, the Contessa cannot travel anywhere without her collection of cuddly toys. Two of the suitcases in the boot are full of soft toys. Zenobia is a darling, but does have to be very careful about her eyes. That's why she wears the glasses. She's a sort of natural hypnotist, and of course, the men . . . well, they *do* get a little unruly on moonlit nights! Zio Giovanni has been married twice, but he's a widower again now. It's very sad.'

'His poor wives,' said Filomena, 'probably died of exhaustion. So much charm is very tiring. I don't even know if I have the strength to trampoline today. That Zio Giovanni quite wore me out.'

Auntie Varvara looked wistfully out of the window.

'Didn't Remo look wonderful? Oh, I'm just longing, longing, longing for my wedding day. It's going to be the happiest day of my life. You've all been so wonderful,' (tears sprang into her eyes) 'and worked so hard that I know it's going to be perfection from start to finish!'

Arnold Peaswallop turned out to be as good a photographer as Auntie Varvara said he was. Rosie was spoiled for choice when it came to picking a representative photograph to put on the Family Wall. In the end, she settled on two. One shows what I now think of as The Gathering of the Clans: all the Fantoras and Lupinos together in a happy group, under the overhanging vines of Eddie's Italian trellis. Everyone looks happy, everyone looks handsome or pretty, depending on their gender, and I myself look better than ever, and what is more, I am right in the forefront of the picture, which is pleasing. The second photograph is of The Happy Couple. Magazines such as the ones to which Auntie Varvara is addicted, say over and over again that every bride is beautiful, and perhaps they are right. Certainly, Auntie Varvara will never look better. Her eyes are sparkling, her cheeks are blushing delicately, her dress is resplendent, her flowers glow with colour ... oh, the whole effect is splendid. Remo is looking at her with adoration, which is only right and proper. He too is looking impressive. Serenity is the order of the day, which only goes to show how the camera can hide the truth as well as reveal it. There were many times during those memorable hours when 'flustered' would have been the word to describe us all. I am drawing a deep breath, and embarking on my account of the Great Day.

The Wedding

Newspapers, which are supposed to provide information, are often content to print only the barest possible outline. On the Monday morning after Auntie Varvara's wedding, this is the paragraph that appeared under a photograph of all of us that was more than usually smudgy, grey and indistinct:

'The marriage of Miss Varvara Fantora took place on Saturday, June 26th, at Barton Bridge Registry Office. The reception was held at 58, Azalea Avenue. Miss Fantora is the sister of Mr Edward Fantora, greengrocer and florist. The bride wore an unusual ensemble in shot silk, and was attended by her nieces and nephew. The couple will honeymoon in New York, and make their home in Italy.'

To read this paragraph is to remain quite ignorant of what actually happened on the day. To peer at the newspaper's idea of a photograph is to miss entirely the splendour of each separate garment. The word 'reception' hardly does justice to what went on in the garden of our house. Luckily, I am here to tell the full story, beginning even before the great day itself dawned.

I don't suppose there would have been much peaceful sleeping in 58, Azalea Avenue on the night before the wedding even without Remo. We were all much too excited. Rosie was pacing the kitchen, opening and shutting cupboard doors, Eddie was fiddling about in the garden, putting the finishing touches to vine trellises (laden with grapes) he had already arranged there. The children were being giggly and restless in Bianca and Francesca's room, playing a game of weddings with Sandy, Candy, Shandy and some of Marco's soldiers. Auntie Varvara was checking to make sure she had 'something old, something new, something borrowed, something blue'. Her hair was set on fat pink rollers with a net over them to keep them neat. Filomena was knitting and shaking her head.

'This,' she said, 'is the busiest and most colour-ful Fair Isle I've done in years. Seventeen colours so far . . . a little bit of almost everything.'

'No bad omens, I hope,' said Auntie Varvara.

'No, no, nothing you wouldn't expect on a big occasion like a wedding . . . the odd bobble every now and then . . . it's only to be expected.'

Filomena looked at Auntie Varvara. 'Don't you think you'd better get to bed? You don't want to be exhausted on your own wedding day . . . and I can still hear noises from the girls' room. Those children . . . they're overexcited. I'd better go and calm them down.'

It was then that the pink Cadillac screeched into Azalea Avenue at high speed. I saw it before anyone else at all, because I had fled from the frantic toings and froings indoors to settle myself on the wall at the front of the house. Remo was at the wheel. He jumped out of the car, slammed the door shut, and proceeded to serenade Auntie Varvara in the dulcet tones of an Italian moved by love. He had no musical accompaniment. He needed none. His voice soared up into the sky, sweet as ice-cream, throbbing with emotion. Now, the residents of Azalea Avenue are not used to serenaders. Ghetto-blasters they know and can deal with, car radios left on for a few minutes as people get out of cars are a regular feature of life, but no one had ever heard songs sung so passionately, so loudly, so tunefully, right out in the open air.

Auntie Varvara's radiant face appeared at an upper window. She had had the presence of mind to cover her rollers with a fetching headscarf. Faces also appeared at almost every other window in the street, to listen to Remo.

'Fancy!' said Dora Collins. 'Isn't that romantic?'

Mr Collins merely sniffed. Mr Garner came to his front door puffing on his pipe. Mason Garner stretched himself out on his front lawn to listen. After about fifteen minutes of song, Remo blew kisses in Auntie Varvara's direction, sprang into the car, and reversed at breakneck speed out of the cul-de-sac. The neighbours went back to their houses. I went indoors, too, and found the Family discussing Remo's performance.

'What do the words mean?' Francesca wanted to know.

'Oh,' said Auntie Varvara, 'I haven't learned much Italian yet, but it was all the usual things . . . you know . . . beautiful vision of love . . . always . . . forever . . . wings of song . . . my heart's treasure . . . just what you'd expect, really.'

'Lynette Collins next door didn't have anyone to serenade her, did she?' Bianca said.

'Well, people from Barton Bridge don't generally go singing outside other people's houses like that,' said Auntie Varvara. 'That's more of a European custom.'

It was extremely late by the time everyone fell

asleep, and by the time they woke up on the Great Day itself, one thing was clear: the heavens had opened and rain had started to fall from a sky the colour of pencil-leads. It showed no sign of wanting to stop, but pattered down with a persistence that boded ill for vine-trellises, Italian picnics in the garden, dainty shoes, skimpy dresses, unusual flowers and best hats. You could truthfully say that once Auntie Varvara had looked out of the window, the house was filled with wailings and gnashings of teeth.

'Francesca!' she sobbed. 'Oh, Francesca, look at it! Can you do something about the garden? Oh, it's sodden . . . what shall we do?'

Francesca does not like being woken abruptly. She rubbed her eyes crossly and said, 'Can I just have breakfast first? Before I do something?'

'There's no time . . . we've still got to dress . . . the white car's coming at ten . . . oh, hurry Francesca, there's a darling!'

Francesca grumbled and sniffed, but went downstairs and out of the back door in her pyjamas. Perhaps it would have been wiser to let her eat her breakfast before embarking on such an important piece of weather alteration. As it was, it took her a full five minutes to conjure up the sun, and another ten to boost it up to a heat sufficient to begin drying up the garden.

'Will it last till we get back from the Registry Office?' Auntie Varvara wanted to know.

'Oh, yes,' said Francesca, attacking her muesli with enthusiasm. 'I'll give it a burst of extra strength before we go. When are you going to put on your dress, Auntie Varvara? Can I come and watch you dressing?'

'No, dear,' said Auntie Varvara. 'It's to be a surprise, and besides, you'll be dressing yourselves. Madame Liliane will be here any minute to help me get ready.'

For an hour before the white car arrived, 58, Azalea Avenue was transformed into the backstage area of a theatre, with everyone rushing about in their dressing-gowns, peering into mirrors, swirling so that their skirts could stick out, adjusting tight collars, tying belts, doing up buttons, spraying hair, puffing powder over noses, and applying perfumes to every available piece of bare skin. It occurred to me (not for the first time!) that I was lucky to be so elegant in my black fur, which was appropriate for every occasion. Eddie had fled downstairs as soon as he could to get out of the way and Marco had taken up his position on the window-seat in the hall. He was writing a poem as a belated wedding present. I decided that as a Narrator, I should be in the thick of things, so I had settled on Auntie Varvara's bed.

When she was ready, even I had to admit that all the months of preparation and suspense had been well worth while. Auntie Varvara had never looked more radiant. In fact, if I am honest, I have to admit that 'radiant' is not a word that readily springs to mind when describing her. Her complexion is generally rather pale, but today, the make-up brushes had been at work, and her cheeks were delicately pink. Her eyes shone, and her mouth was painted a most enticing shade of scarlet. And the dress ... even my considerable powers of description could never do justice to it. The fabric shimmered and glowed like a million butterfly-wings stitched together, appearing green from one angle, mauve from another, silver from a third. The fabric was draped and hung so that it seemed to move around Auntie Varvara's body like water, flowing and undulating. The skirt was composed of panels of material which ended in long, pointed fronds, edged with seed pearls. Madame Liliane had surpassed herself. The finishing touch was a hat made entirely from stiff net of the palest green, decorated with mauve lace butterflies, which encircled Auntie Varvara's head like a cloud.

Bianca and Francesca stood open-mouthed when they saw her. Their own taffeta dresses, pretty though they undoubtedly were, paled by comparison. Rosie, in maroon brocade, and Filomena in a new costume of deep saffron-yellow clasped their hands together in awe. Filomena had tears in her eyes.

'It's not like me,' she admitted, 'to be so

sentimental, but a daughter getting married is . . .
well . . . special, and you look so lovely.'

Eddie had prepared the bouquet and it was
waiting in the bathroom sink until Auntie Varvara
was dressed. Madame Liliane went to fetch it.

'Such lilies!' she exclaimed. 'Such lilies I have
never seen before. A colour like this is perfect for
the dress.'

'They were grown specially for me,' Auntie
Varvara said. 'And called after me as well.'

The white car arrived at last, decked with ribbons and with a chauffeur at the wheel dressed
all in white. Auntie Varvara was to ride in it with
Eddie and Filomena. Rosie was going in the
Fantora Family car with Bianca, Marco and
Francesca. There was a five-minute delay while
everyone argued about me.

'I'm not going without Ozzy,' said Francesca,
stamping her foot.

'You can't take cats into a Registry Office,'
said Rosie.

'Why not? Monkey and Leopard are coming.'

'Oh, no, they're not.' Rosie was becoming red
in the face. 'Take them back into the house this
very second or you're going to stay home as well,
wedding or no wedding.'

'Can Ozzy come if I take Monkey and Leopard
back?' Francesca pleaded.

'Very well,' said Rosie. 'I haven't got time to
argue. We're late as it is. Hurry up, Francesca.'

Francesca hurried, and soon I found myself sitting on her lap, and on my way to the wedding.

'Ozzy,' she whispered to me as we drove through the streets at a somewhat undignified speed, 'I've done something awful. I've forgotten to give the back garden weather an extra boost. What if the sunshine doesn't last long enough? Auntie Varvara'll kill me. Oh, Ozzy, I'm going to be worried all through the wedding.'

I worried as well, and it nearly spoiled the ceremony for me. I know they say that a trouble shared is a trouble halved, but I wish Francesca hadn't told me. My trouble wasn't halved, but doubled.

'Mum,' said Marco suddenly, 'why are we going so fast? We overtook the white car ages ago. We'll be there long before they are.'

'It's so that Francesca can cheer up the weather round the Registry Office before Auntie Varvara gets there.'

Rosie's car was the first to arrive. There was no sign of the pink Cadillac. We all got out and Bianca held me in her arms. Francesca concentrated on the weather, and soon passers-by were looking up at the sky in amazement. This was surely the smallest sunny interval anyone had ever seen. One side of the street was warm and sunny and on the other the rain was so heavy that it splashed up in little fountains where it hit a puddle.

Auntie Varvara, Eddie and Filomena arrived and still there was no sign of the pink Cadillac. Rosie had phoned the Lupinos' hotel, and was told they had left an hour ago.

'Where *is* he?' wailed Auntie Varvara from the white leather interior of the hired car. 'I'm not getting out and waiting for him in there. The bride is the one who's meant to be late.' She blinked. She couldn't possibly cry and ruin her make-up. 'Let's drive around and see if we can find them. Or just drive round and round until they get here.'

The arrival of Arnold Peaswallop with all his paraphernalia distracted us for a while. He began to fiddle with his bits and pieces, setting up his tripod for what he called 'groups'.

In the end, the Lupinos did arrive, of course, and only half an hour late, although for all of us, every single minute of the thirty seemed like a whole day.

'Scusi,' Zio Giovanni spoke for all of them. 'We have become lost.'

They had taken one wrong turning and were halfway to Oldham before realizing their mistake. Remo had driven as only an Italian in a hurry knows how to drive and here they were at last, the pink Cadillac now spattered all over with brown splashes of mud.

'Carissima!' Remo's yellow eyes glowed when he saw his bride-to-be. 'You forgive me?'

He sank to one knee on the steps of the Registry Office, and kissed Auntie Varvara's hand.

Zenobia was magnificent in orange silk, and the Contessa had chosen oyster-coloured lace for her wedding outfit. She stood on the steps waving regally at passers-by.

'Is that the Queen Mother?' squeaked one little girl.

'Don't be silly,' said her mother. 'That's just someone going to a wedding.'

Zio Giovanni sidled up to Filomena, and tucked her arm into his.

'You are more beautiful than the bride,' he murmured.

'And you are a wicked old man,' Filomena said happily, 'telling such dreadful lies!'

The ceremony itself was mercifully short. Bianca put me down on a chair near the door, from where I had a splendid view of the proceedings. Bianca amused herself by bringing to life the lace butterflies on Auntie Varvara's hat. They flitted around the room, and one of them settled on the shoulder of the Registrar himself. He looked a little disconcerted, but carried on regardless as though nothing had happened. Rosie glared at Bianca, but it was too late. Francesca was fretting. Only I knew what she was fretting about and I fretted with her to keep her company.

After the ceremony was over, Arnold Peaswallop took some photographs of the happy couple, and of the whole family. None of these has found its way on to the Family Wall, because he managed to catch us all at the wrong moments: the Contessa cross-eyed with looking at a butterfly that had landed briefly on her nose, Remo with his tongue sticking out a little as he signed the wedding certificate, Zio Giovanni winking at Filomena, and Francesca looking very worried indeed. I was sure things would improve when we got back to 58, Azalea Avenue, and they did.

We came home with seconds to spare as far as the weather in the garden was concerned. Already, clouds had covered the sun, and begun to puff out into alarming grey shapes in the sky. Francesca ran to the garden, and sent them scurrying away with one glance. The sun beamed down undisturbed once more. The guests began to arrive and very soon, we were all in the garden.

'You have made us a garden like in Italy!' the Contessa exclaimed when she saw it. 'How beautiful! Grazie!'

She flung her arms round Eddie, who blushed as red as the roses in Auntie Varvara's bouquet. The garden was indeed transformed. The vines on the trellises were heavy with purple grapes, there were cypress trees in pots, and marble statues dotted here and there. ('Not real marble, Ozzy,' Eddie had confessed. 'Just imitations from the Garden Centre, but quite effective in the right setting.') The table stretched the whole length of the lawn, and was piled high with salads, and small, bite-sized morsels of delicious things looking like small jewels on enormous china plates. There were white slices of chicken breast, and pink slices of salmon. There were bowls full of mayonnaise, cut-glass dishes overflowing with plump asparagus, and baskets bursting with strawberries. In the very centre of the table was The Cake: four tiers of it, rising like a pink and white mountain from the folds of the tablecloth, and at the very top, models of Auntie Varvara and Remo at the door of their sugar castle.

I never realized that Auntie Varvara had so many friends. The garden was so full of people that hardly anyone noticed Monkey and Leopard prowling among the forest of legs, looking for dropped titbits. Leopard managed to chew a considerable number of holes in the Contessa's skirt without her noticing. He evidently had a taste for lace we knew nothing about.

Arnold Peaswallop had been entranced by Zenobia. She had taken her dark glasses off, just for a moment, and fixed him with her topaz eyes, and now he was mesmerized, wandering after her through the crowds with a dazed look on his face, and his mouth hanging open. From time to time, he remembered what he had been engaged to do, and he aimed his camera at this or that group of people but it became necessary for

Zenobia herself to cajole him into posing the more formal wedding portraits. Bianca spotted two of the Contessa's cuddly toys (a beige giraffe and a pinkish elephant) nestling on the back seat of the Cadillac, and she had sent Marco to fetch the keys from Remo, and taken them out.

'It's only fair they should be at the wedding, too,' she said, and brought them to life.

The Contessa needed a reviving glass of champagne when she first saw them running about, but she soon grew so excited by the idea of living cuddly toys that she begged Bianca to come to Italy and use her magic on the whole collection. Perhaps by now the Contessa will have had time to regret the idea. I, for one, tremble at the thought of any dwelling, even a palazzo, being overrun by hundreds of furry, woolly, fluffy and mostly pastel-coloured creatures.

I have to admit to falling asleep and missing all the speeches. I woke up just in time to see Auntie Varvara (dressed now in chic black and white stripes) depart for her honeymoon, after tossing her bouquet into the air and laughing uproariously when it was Filomena who caught it. She and Remo walked down the front path to where the taxi awaited them. A crowd of mixed Fantoras and Lupinos followed them down to the gate. There was much kissing. There were tears. Hankies were brought out. Sniffs were heard. The word 'goodbye' echoed all around, and at last they were gone, off to sample the delights of New York.

'We go back now,' said Zio Giovanni, noticing how weepy Filomena had become, 'and make the party. We sing, we dance . . . till morning. We are all happy!'

The party went on for hours. There was nowhere a poor cat could rest his head undisturbed. Arnold Peaswallop and Zenobia found what must have been the last quiet corner for their murmurings and canoodlings. Zio Giovanni told stories of the old days, and burbled songs into Filomena's ear, Rosie and the Contessa discussed children and plants and food and remembered other weddings. They also began to plan for the holiday that is now drawing to an end. A special toast was drunk to Francesca, who made the sun shine so brightly, but she had fallen asleep long ago and been taken up to bed. Marco and Bianca also went upstairs in the end.

Marco said, 'I never showed Auntie Varvara my poem.'

'You can send it to her in a letter,' said Bianca, 'and in the morning you can show it to us.'

We all thought the poem was so appropriate that we hung it up on the Family Wall in the same frame as the wedding group. I am reading it now, to remind myself of an exhilarating and exhausting day.

You are marrying today.
All the Family want to say
a very loud hip hip hooray
to dearest Auntie Varvara.

Your dress will be the best dress yet,
your hair will be all washed and set
and lovely presents you will get,
Oh dearest Auntie Varvara.

We'll eat lots of wedding cake,
lots of photographs we'll take,
people will long speeches make
to dearest Auntie Varvara.

We wish you love, hugs and a kiss,
tons and tons of married bliss,
but alas, we're going to miss
our dearest Auntie Varvara.

The Family are returning to Azalea Avenue tomorrow. I can hardly wait to see them. Soon the quiet that has settled round me will be gone. Eddie will be knocking nails into the Family Wall, and Rosie will be deciding which of the holidays snaps is good enough to deserve a place among the Fantora Family Photographs.

Filomena's Colour Chart

Remember that all the colours can mean many different things, depending on the combinations in which they are found. This is because life is never only one thing at a time.

RED   When dark, it means anger, violence, blood.
When lighter, it means annoyance and minor irritations.

YELLOW   Means happiness, wealth and sunshine.

APRICOT/
PEACH   Means comfort, luxury, and good food.

ORANGE   Means very hot weather, but also fire.

GREEN   Means either: new life and growth (PALE GREEN)
or: illness and bad luck (LIME GREEN)
or: jealousy (EMERALD GREEN)
A certain shade of BLUEY-GREEN means weddings.

BLUE   Means either: unhappiness (DEEP ROYAL BLUE)
or: peace (GREENY–BLUE)
or: anger (PURPLY–BLUE)
or: travel (PALE BLUE)
or: sleep (NAVY BLUE)
or: water (GREY–BLUE)

BLACK   Means revenge, blindness, night-time.
Mixed with white it means bad weather.

GREY/
BEIGE   Are the colours of Ordinary Life and change their
meaning as bits of other colours are added to them.

PINK   Means affection. DEEP PINK means Love, and if blue
is added to pink to make MAUVE it means Unhappy
Love

PURPLE/
DEEP
MAUVE   Means Pain. Intensity varies from the MAUVE of
bruises to the DEEP PURPLE of very severe pain.

BROWN   Is the colour of Earth.

GOLD   Is the colour of Friendship.

SILVER   Is the colour of Air and the Imagination.

WHITE   Is the colour of Death.